Using Portfolios

Kathy McClelland, Ph.D.
Auburn University

LONGMAN

An Imprint of Addison Wesley Longman, Inc.

New York • Reading, Massachusetts • Menlo Park, California • Harlow, England
Don Mills, Ontario • Sydney • Mexico City • Madrid • Amsterdam

Using Portfolios

Copyright © 2001 Longman Publishers USA, a division of Addison Wesley Longman, Inc.

ISBN: 0-321-08412-8

12345678910-DM-03020100

CONTENTS

Preface   iii

Chapter 1:
    What are portfolios, exactly? Will I have
    to change the way I teach?   1

Chapter 2:
    Why use portfolios?   15

Chapter 3:
    What goes into portfolios? And how do I
    introduce portfolio evaluation to students?   41

Chapter 4:
    Evaluating portfolios   53

Chapter 5:
    Electronic portfolios   79

Sources   91

Postscript   95

PREFACE

WHAT ISN'T IN THIS BOOK

If you are looking for a scholarly, fully-documented, and philosophical discussion of portfolio use in composition at the college level, you've picked up the wrong book. Though I have included some references to some of the literature and the better-known names in assessment and portfolio use in particular, I have chosen not to go into the kind of detail you might be looking for. You won't find a comprehensive list of resources, either; the one I offer consists of sources I've found most helpful over the years. I won't even claim that this book is comprehensive; I don't cover all the possibilities for how to use portfolios. Nor will you find exhaustive or extensive examples of portfolios here.

WHAT IS IN THIS BOOK, THEN?

What I offer you here are some of my thoughts and ideas concerning portfolio evaluation. I have tried to explain some of the basic reasons, processes, and materials I use in portfolio evaluation in freshman composition courses. Most of what follows describes my solutions to some problems and attitudes I encountered as I developed as a teacher of writing and the materials I have developed and use on a regular basis. Thanks to Angela Insenga, a generous GTA (Graduate Teaching Assistant), I've also been able to include some alternative samples and ideas as well.

I've tried to cover portfolios from some very basic perspectives:

> - In Chapter 1, I describe portfolios in general, a bit about their current use, how they fit into the scheme of evaluation in different levels of education. I have focused specifically, however, on how they fit into the context of the college-level composition class and how activities in such a class might change.

> - In Chapter 2, I discuss some theoretical and personal reasons for using portfolio evaluation in the college-level composition class and how students tend to respond to portfolio evaluation and why. I have included some ideas on why and how using portfolio evaluation benefits students and teachers, as well as some of the disadvantages in using portfolio evaluation for both teachers and students.

> - In Chapter 3, I describe kinds of portfolios and the possible contents of composition portfolios, the nuts and bolts of keeping track of the contents, record keeping changes, and how I ask students to set them up.

> - In Chapter 4, I explain the practical how-to-determine final grades, how to match the evaluation to a departmental rubric or requirements, and how students should become involved in the evaluation process.

> - In Chapter 5, I share some suggestions and observations about using portfolios in a computerized environment.

Interspersed throughout are samples of various forms and information sheets I have used; look for the boxed material labeled as samples. I offer them in the hope that you will be able to adapt them to fit your individual needs, tastes, programmatic requirements, and voice.

You will even be able to use this book to determine whether portfolios might work for you. In all instances where I list requirements or attitudes, you'll see the bullet is actually a small box. The more of those boxes you can check in each list, the more you have an indication that portfolios might work for you.

WHO AM I?

But let me introduce myself first; after all, you don't know me, and you don't know why I can claim some expertise at portfolio evaluation.

First and foremost, I am a teacher of writing; specifically, I teach freshman composition courses and have for over twenty years. And, for all but the first few years, I've used some kind of portfolio evaluation.

As a composition teacher, I work strictly from a process-based philosophy: I don't believe I can teach anyone to write, but I can provide opportunities (usually in the form of problems to be solved) that will allow students to learn to write if they take advantage of them. The best way for me to do that is to set up a community of writers and readers who work together to achieve certain goals (in our case, a final portfolio that meets programmatic requirements) over the course of a term. I serve as the coach, the guide, the experienced reader/writer who helps by introducing options, offering suggestions, and negotiating choices.

But, as the assistant to the Coordinator of Composition in a large English department, I am also involved in training new GTAs to teach our freshman composition courses. We have very little time to get them ready to walk into the classroom on the first day of classes, never mind the finer points of teaching, so we have to cover the basics early and work with them as they teach their first class.

Other than having something prepared for class everyday, the hardest aspect of teaching that our GTAs face is grading papers. We do some work with practice papers before the actual teaching begins, and we do more training when they have their first set of papers to evaluate. Frustration with using the departmental grading rubric usually sets in as the GTAs discover that grading asks them to make judgments they don't want to make. Quite often, GTAs will want to use grades as punishment for poor effort (e.g., when students don't write a draft or don't actively engage in peer response), for what they consider grammatical and mechanical error, and even when students choose to revise some aspect of a paper differently from the way the GTA has told them to. Some GTAs will go the other direction, wanting to reward student efforts in revision; the paper usually gets an inflated grade. We always end up discussing how the rubric must be applied to the text of the final paper, only. So, what about the other issues? How do they count in the grade? When they ask for alternatives, I find myself explaining portfolio evaluation. Inevitably the GTAs ask, "Can't we do portfolio grading, too?"

"Yes and no" is the official answer. No, because teachers need to become familiar with the function and role of evaluation and grading early in their teaching, and this department believes the traditional grading methods work best for that. I tend to agree; learning to apply the rubric fairly and consistently is important for beginning teachers. But, after their first year of teaching, the GTAs interested in portfolio evaluation are invited to take a special seminar training them to use portfolios; if they do so, they are allowed to adopt the practice their second year. The seminar is considered extra-curricular and voluntary, but it is required if they want to use portfolio evaluation. I teach it at their request.

This book has grown out of the materials I use in that seminar and material I have developed over the years as I have worked to refine my practice of portfolio evaluation.

WHY DO I USE PORTFOLIOS?

The answer is pretty simple: I was ready to give up teaching when grading papers started beating me up. After a few years of hearing "Why did you give me a C on this paper?" and "What do I have to do to make it an A paper?" in conferences where I would try to discuss options for revision, I adopted portfolios as a survival mechanism.

I wasn't teaching writing the way I knew I needed to and the way I wanted to. The students' concerns (grades, specifically, but also that nagging need to know how to do it right or how to do it the way I wanted it) were impinging far too often. I just got tired of the authority students insisted I accept. I didn't want it; I wanted them to accept the responsibility for their choices, not depend on me to tell them what to do to achieve that almighty A on a paper. Colleagues were beginning to use portfolios, so I tried them, too. To say that I was delighted with the results and that I changed as a teacher and learner are both understatements. I've never gone back to traditional grading methods, and I've continued to refine my teaching using portfolio evaluation.

Solving these problems of writing to the grade, of focusing on what is right, of not really learning anything about writing was the biggest impetus for me to use portfolios. But I'm getting ahead of myself; I'll come back to this point in Chapter 2, Why Use Portfolios?

WHO IS THIS BOOK FOR?

Anyone teaching composition or writing-based courses might find this information useful, but I have specifically kept GTAs, instructors new to teaching composition, and instructors who are looking for an alternative to traditional grading systems in mind. I'm assuming that GTAs might be given the chance to use portfolios as they develop their own styles of teaching, that instructors having to teach composition for the first time might not have had theory and practice courses covering evaluation with portfolios and want to know about it, and that some experienced teachers of composition are having the same problems I used to and want to find an alternative to traditional grading practices.

WHY GTAS AND INSTRUCTORS
NEW TO COMPOSITION?

GTAs tend to discover early that, when learning to teach in a process-oriented course where revision is important, some ideas seem contradictory when they also have to learn to negotiate the relative importance of various requirements spelled out in the departmental grading rubric. That is, the means of achieving goals and the quality of the results don't always seem to reinforce each other. At least that's what some of the GTAs in our department report. But once they figure out that grading a paper is different from evaluating a student's writing ability (which is what I maintain a grade in a writing course should reflect), I suspect they will want an alternative. I'm hoping that GTAs and instructors new to teaching composition might find some information that will help them develop their own teaching philosophy, develop their own sense of the role of and the importance of grading and evaluation within the program they find themselves.

In addition, I know these teachers will want to find ways to make their experiences a bit easier; after all, the challenges of planning and teaching a brand new course is often terribly time-consuming. Just the day-to-day demands of preparing class materials take time GTAs rarely have when they are working in their own graduate courses.

And, teachers new to composition but who have taught other kinds of courses might find that composition makes different kinds of demands on their evaluation procedures; assessing writing ability is fundamentally different from evaluating the quality of an essay exam answer or even a multiple choice test on literature.

WHY MIGHT EXPERIENCED TEACHERS WANT TO CONSIDER USING PORTFOLIOS?

If any of the following statements describe you, I suspect you are ready to consider using portfolio evaluation:

- ❑ I am frustrated by programmatic requirements that focus on product when I know I need to focus on process.

- ❑ I am more interested in allowing learning to happen that I am in students writing to a grade.

- ❑ I don't value hoop-jumping; that is, I really hate to hear the phrases "just tell me what you want" or "she seems to like narratives; use a lot of those" from my students.

- ❑ I want to give students a voice in their own learning and evaluation.

- ❑ I want students to make their own choices, not to depend on me to tell them how to "do it right."

❑ I am math-challenged and resent the time I spend with a calculator at the end of each term. Besides, I'm not sure I can quantify writing ability.

Each of these statements reflects some aspect of teaching writing that seems to impose a negative influence on what we do in the classroom to achieve the goals set forth by a program or a department. Each statement echoes one of my personal reasons for moving to portfolio evaluation. Each also represents a potential area of contention you might face within your specific teaching environment; these are the areas you'll find yourself negotiating and defending as you move toward using portfolios.

I doubt you'll be able to move into portfolio grading overnight; you'll want to be prepared for intense conversations and the need to compromise. Your colleagues will need to understand how portfolios evaluated with a rubric based on the departmental one will reflect the standards they use. I'll explain more about this compromise in Chapter 3, How to Evaluate Portfolios.

THE BOTTOM LINE

Basically, this book is an offering from someone who has used portfolios for years, who couldn't go back to traditional grading if she had to, and who is interested, ultimately, in allowing students to learn to write. I hope you'll discover information that might be useful as you try to decide whether portfolios fit into your philosophy of teaching writing. If you do, I hope you'll find the answers to some fundamental questions about how to implement and use portfolios successfully.

A WORD OF WARNING (OF SORTS)

Using portfolio evaluation is as much a way of teaching as it is a means of assessment. Teachers who use portfolios have to make some major adjustments to traditional practices:

- ❑ No more grade books (but you do have to keep good records!).

- ❑ No quizzes, no tests (at least I don't; students write instead), except, in my case, for the departmental exam, which becomes another piece of writing in the portfolio for us.

- ❑ No numbers (check marks if they did it, an X if they didn't, and a holistic reading of all of it at the end; I've included a sample of my record sheet later in the text).

- ❑ Fewer long nights or weekends spent grading papers (which isn't such a bad thing!).

Ultimately, you might decide portfolios are not that much better for students or easier for you, given your individual situation. Why? Because there are different kinds of demands for your time and attention:

- ❑ Lots more reading (if it is important for me to assign, for them to write, I can at least do them the courtesy of reading it), especially in a short period at the end of the term.

- ❑ Lots more writing (I don't evaluate any piece, but I do comment as I read), both during the term and especially at the end of the term when I get portfolios.

- ❑ Lots more talking (conferencing has become a staple in my practice).

For me, the trade offs work, but you'll have to judge for yourself. I'll cover more of the nuts and bolts issues of how all this happens in Chapter 4, but I'll share tips about how to accomplish these as I go. Look for *Practical Suggestions* (and a few personal comments in boxes in the text, like the one here.

> ## *PS*
>
> These boxes have information I hope you'll find valuable, but much of which experienced teachers will already know. I've also indulged myself at times and shared a few stories and observations I hope you find thought provoking.

CHAPTER 1

WHAT ARE PORTFOLIOS, EXACTLY?
WILL I HAVE TO CHANGE THE WAY I TEACH?

The principle of a portfolio is basic, whatever the contents; it is a body of work collected and maintained for the purpose of representing the keeper's abilities and achievements.

For the composition teacher, the portfolio is the record of all the material that a student writes over the course of a term; this includes everything from journals to homework assignments to drafts of papers to revisions to responses to others' writing to the final papers themselves.

Those are my definitions, but the ones you'll read in any dictionary or reference book will be similar. Portfolios for a college composition class work much the same way as they do in any other situation; they represent a writer's best efforts at responses to assignments.

A (VERY) BRIEF REVIEW OF PORTFOLIO USE

Portfolios have a long history in disciplines other than composition. Banking, finance, and money management systems traditionally refer to holdings of stocks, bonds, and accounts as *portfolios*. Diplomats in government service are often said to be *with portfolio* or credentials. Artists, advertising companies, writers, and publishers all maintain representative holdings they consider portfolios.

Portfolios are being used more and more in the educational setting at all levels as teachers learn to value the learning process over the product-oriented or even a test-based curriculum. Portfolio use in writing courses, especially, evolved partially out of the frustration educators experienced with large-scale assessment issues. Writing teachers recognized early that a one-shot, statistically valid and reliable test was close to impossible to develop. But arguments for portfolios didn't enter the major literature focusing on composition (a sure sign that something is becoming a major aspect of the field) until the late 1970s and early 1980s. The Belanoff and Elbow article "Using Portfolios to Increase Collaboration and Community in a Writing Program" in the Spring 1986 edition of *Writing Program Administration* is one of the earliest to discuss using portfolios on a programmatic level.

Some teachers had been using the *writing folder* before that, but using portfolios as an assessment tool for the classroom teacher has become popular only in the last twenty years. Lots has happened in that time; portfolios have been used as a means of large-scale assessment (see Belanoff and Elbow; Belanoff and Dickson; Yancy), and teachers have begun using them in classes as an alternative to traditional grading practices. Most recently, thanks to developments in computer technology and the widespread accessibility of the World Wide Web, electronic portfolios are becoming more and more popular.

HOW PORTFOLIOS WORK

The crux of portfolio evaluation is timing. Evaluation happens when it is appropriate, after the students have had the chance to

2

practice material introduced. In most cases, nothing a student writes during the term is graded; instead, he/she works toward submitting a body of work at the end of the term.

At issue, too, is the whole concept of what we evaluate. That is, are we really looking at what a student has learned? Or are we checking to see whether he or she has jumped the correct hoops to achieve the grade all students want, the A? I know that portfolios show me what a student has learned by allowing me to see how he has applied it.

I think the best way for me to explain the basics of portfolio evaluation is to show you how portfolios work in an elementary classroom.

In elementary schools, teachers are using portfolios to assess learning by tracing the development of reading, writing, and math ability. I know of one first grade teacher whose students are responsible for maintaining a file of all their work. A large file box in one corner of the classroom holds special folders; each child is responsible for filing any assessment or test and any other piece of work he or she thinks is a good example of his or her efforts. Assessments (tests) of math and phonics are kept in the portfolio; the teacher keeps a separate writing portfolio. Over the course of any grading period, the students are free to add to either portfolio any paper they think is especially good.

At the end of the first grading period, each student reviews the contents of the portfolio with the teacher, discussing efforts, achievements, and what the grades actually mean (O is outstanding, meaning almost perfect work; S is satisfactory, meaning things are fine for now; and I means needs improvement), and what the student thinks the appropriate grade for each subject area, basing his or her grade on the portfolio contents; the teacher then fills out the report card with the child's supervision.

3

By the end of the third reporting period, students are able to evaluate their own work and explain in writing why they think they deserve the grade they propose. After the teacher reviews this self-evaluation and conferences with the student if she disagrees with the self-assessment (they have to come to an agreement), she reviews the portfolio and the student's self-assessment with the parents. What do parents think? This teacher sends a letter, explaining portfolio evaluation, to the parents at the end of the first grading period. She reports that in five years of using this system, no parent has ever complained.

Is it really possible for first graders to assess their own abilities? Apparently so; the teacher reports the students understand that grades indicate a measure of success and that at least nine out of ten children assess themselves at the level she would. No one gets upset with his or her report card, and parents seem to appreciate the fact that their child has a clear understanding of his or her abilities.

PORTFOLIOS AT OTHER GRADE LEVELS

This same process of placing the responsibility for maintaining the portfolio, participating in the evaluation, and keeping parents informed is useful for teachers in junior and senior high schools who are using portfolios. Finding references to teachers using portfolios in science and history classes, as well as English/writing portfolios, is quite easy if you search the literature and the Web. Some high school systems are adopting portfolio assessment as graduation criteria; Kentucky, for instance, has instituted an exit portfolio as part of high school graduation requirements.

At the collegiate level, English departments with process-oriented composition programs are using them in several ways, most often, perhaps, as a means of program assessment or in place of proficiency tests. Belanoff and Elbow were among the first to propose this use at SUNY Stony Brook, and several other schools have followed their example.

But, many colleges and universities have retained the more traditional means of assessing programs and even student performance. Students write papers teachers assign, and teachers grade papers based on some ideal they have in mind. As more and more individual teachers who work from a process-oriented philosophy join the faculty at these schools, however, we see more and more teachers using portfolio evaluation in their classes.

IN THE COLLEGE COMPOSITION CLASS

Though portfolio evaluation has been a standard for me for several years, I still find that I am among the few who uses it in a writing class outside the technical and business writing focus. Teachers of those classes (who are lucky since their curricula enjoy a more specified and real-world orientation) seem to have moved into portfolio evaluation much more readily than freshman composition teachers have. But as a process-oriented curriculum becomes more the norm of

> **PS**
> A process-oriented writing curriculum isn't necessary for portfolio evaluation, however. Student writing in any class would be appropriate for portfolio evaluation.

composition courses at the college level, more and more instances of portfolio evaluation are surfacing.

In my composition classes, portfolios become, in a way, a physical goal; that is, all our efforts are somehow tied to developing the contents of the portfolio. And, because I teach in a program with a fairly-specifically defined curriculum (mainly to ensure some sort

5

of programmatic consistency), most of the contents of the portfolio are decided for me. However, I have students keep track of everything they do over the course of the term, so the portfolio also becomes a developmental record as well. In addition to the final papers (determined by the curriculum), I get to see the daily work, drafts, responses, revisions, and everything else associated with the course.

Paramount, however, are the final papers that students work toward over the course of the quarter. The process approach, coupled with portfolio evaluation, allows me to have time to work with students as they

❑ prewrite: we do some in class the day they get the assignment;

❑ draft: on their own, with the encouragement to make it as solid as possible

❑ participate in a peer response session: usually guided and paper specific after we discuss how and why to respond as real readers;

❑ revise: focusing on both peer comments and my sense of what general weaknesses I see in a file copy;

❑ conference with me: to see how the writer has addressed peer comments and to add my suggestions for (other kinds of) revision;

❑ revise again;

❑ get more response: from me, from consultants in our English Center, from peers;

- revise again, and get more response (as many times as they wish);

- craft (cleaning up the prose; working on word choice, diction level, etc.);

- prepare the final draft (some call it the presentation copy);

> **PS**
>
> Have students initial the corner of the final drafts to indicate that they have proofread their papers.

- edit (yes, on the pages submitted, with a black pen, catching mistakes that spell check and grammar check didn't).

That is, portfolios allow me to offer the time students need to develop a truly recursive writing process. Rather than having to evaluate a paper that has gone through a more-or-less linear process with maybe one response/revision loop in it, students in my portfolio class can actually practice the more real recursive process of writing; they can revise and get responses (from me, the consultants in the English Center, even their peer group members) as many times as they wish.

In addition, I have more time to discuss rhetorical concerns; that is, I don't have to cover everything from global revision to editing before they submit their first paper.

CHANGES IN CLASSROOM ACTIVITIES

In all honesty, there are very few. The syllabus the program suggests (based on the modified process I described above) we use fits my efforts to allow additional revision opportunities as well. What changes I do see are beneficial ones.

More prewriting

Instead of handing out the assignment, reviewing it, and answering questions, I can take time to have students engage in specific prewriting activities during class. Often these take the form of talk in peer groups, allowing students to discuss ideas, focus, audience, rhetorical constraints, and questions about the assignment.

I usually ask for a journal entry (a five-minute freewrite) that sums up the decisions students have made before they leave; reading these allows me to frame comments and answers to questions for the next class. I can point out danger zones, make recommendations, share suggestions about focus, etc. Most students tell me that they like these journal entries when they discover how useful they are when writing the papers.

More peer review opportunities

Instead of just one peer review session per paper, I am often able to work in two, one on an early draft and one on a nearly completed revision, and sometimes more. Some students will even take the opportunity to meet outside of class to work on drafts, especially toward the end of the term.

More conferencing opportunities

I require that students meet with me in one conference per paper, but given that they can revise as often as they wish, students (the ones committed to the process, anyway) are free to (and encouraged to) visit during office hours or make appointments for us to review more developed drafts. Sometimes they merely want confirmation that they have done well and for me to tell them the paper is complete; I won't do that, however. For each required conference and each successive one, everyone must explain specifically where and what kind(s) of problem(s) they are encountering so I can tailor my comments and our discussion. This also means they have to take the responsibility of critiquing their own work and deciding where they see weaknesses.

Sample 1.1 on pages 10 and 11 is a form I sometimes use to help them do this; everyone brings this form, completed as best he or she can, to the required conference. I have completed the same one; we compare our responses and negotiate revision suggestions if need be. I usually use the same form for additional response conferences on revisions. The checklist might seem mechanical, and I hate having to use it for that reason, but students report finding it valuable. I've even had classes ask for a checklist to use on the final exam (which I don't respond to, but which they can conduct peer responses sessions for).

Sample #1.1: Response Checklist

Response Checklist ("I" = reader; "you" = writer)

FOCUS
- ❑ Seems too broad/general
- ❑ Seems too narrow/specific
- ❑ Seems about right
- ❑ Doesn't seem to be one

POINT/THESIS
- ❑ Is not clear: I don't know what your point is
- ❑ Is weak: you're telling info, but I'm not sure what connection you have to it
- ❑ Seems more for you than for readers
- ❑ Seems pretty contrived, like you're doing an assignment you really don't want to do
- ❑ Is clear to me

PURPOSE
- ❑ Is confusing: I don't see what you're driving at
- ❑ Is weak: you're telling info, but I'm not sure why it should be important to me
- ❑ Is not evident: you are telling info, but I don't know why
- ❑ Is clear to me

INTRO
- ❑ There isn't one; I am thrust right into the middle of the situation
- ❑ Is pretty minimal; I could use some additional help here
- ❑ Is formulaic; any way to spice it up?
- ❑ Introduces topic & gets me interested
- ❑ Is too long and involved

BODY
- ❑ Is confusing; many paragraphs are very general
- ❑ Is confusing; I don't see relationships between paragraphs, point
- ❑ Is confusing; I need paragraph transitions
- ❑ Is weak; I need more examples, explanation, connections
- ❑ Does not seem to be about the topic discussed in the introduction → I'm confused!
- ❑ Seems to be working ok for me as it is now

CONCLUSION
- ❏ There isn't one
- ❏ Doesn't match the intro → I'm confused!
- ❏ Seems pretty formulaic
- ❏ Seems pretty abrupt
- ❏ Seems to introduce a new topic
- ❏ Ties things up ok for now
- ❏ Ties things up pretty well

EXAMPLES/EVIDENCE/SUPPORT
- ❏ I don't really get much
- ❏ I get some, but it seems too general in spots
- ❏ I get enough, but could use more
- ❏ I need more specifics all the way through
- ❏ I think you're depending too much on one
- ❏ I could use some different kind of examples

Voice/Style/Tone
- ❏ I don't really hear a voice in this
- ❏ The voice seems too impersonal
- ❏ The voice seems too personal
- ❏ The voice is appropriate
- ❏ The style is too formal/academic
- ❏ The style is too informal
- ❏ The style is not academic
- ❏ The style is appropriate
- ❏ The tone is too harsh
- ❏ The tone is too noncommittal
- ❏ The tone is appropriate

The biggest problem area(s)/the aspect(s) to focus on in revising is (are):
- ❏ Focus
- ❏ Point
- ❏ Purpose
- ❏ Intro
- ❏ Body
- ❏ Conclusion
- ❏ Examples, evidence

Specific Revision suggestions:

Yes, this means I do more reading and more conferencing, but my response occurs only in a conference (A confession: I gave up writing extensive comments on papers long ago). I still do marginalia, but I discuss weaknesses and make suggestion in conferences, and I insist the student be responsible for writing down the comments and ideas. Why? When they record our comments and suggestions, they will use their language; most report they remember it better this way. Even more important is the concept of

PS

Conferences will go faster and you'll be able to accomplish more if you can read each paper and do marginal comments the night before. I've discovered that I can retain enough of the paper to be able to spend the entire conference time talking, not reading the draft.

ownership. When I write everything down for them, I own the revision; that is, they know I have done the work of recording thinking for them. When they have to write our comments down, they have to accept ownership of the ideas I suggest to them. As I read the revisions in preparation for the conference, all I need to do is jot notes to myself that address the issue(s) the student has identified as problematic. That doesn't take so long, and inevitably during the conference, we discover even more possibilities for improving the draft.

More formal instruction of rhetorical elements ~ Mini-lessons

Mini-lessons become a distinct focus and almost daily occurrence of classroom instruction for me; I can address one aspect of writing at a time as they work on the papers. This means I don't have to cover editing concerns early on (when the first paper is due in other classes, for example); I have found that when I do that, grammar and mechanics take over as the focus of the course and the students' writing. Instead, I can discuss global concerns of focus, development of ideas, organization, and overall coherence.

By mid-term, our mini-lessons address issues of paragraph transitions, paragraph development, and sources of evidence. By the end of the term, we are discussing surface issues of active/passive verbs, parallelism, and sentence combining for flow and pace.

On course evaluations, some students comment that they wish we had mini-lessons earlier; those are the students who haven't really tapped into the possibility of revision as the term progresses, the ones who want to finish one paper before starting another. I understand that need, however, so I have started incorporating some typically later mini-lessons earlier in the term. I use the weaknesses I see in their drafts to tell me which.

ONE LAST THOUGHT

Using portfolio evaluation means some of the typical activities in a class are different, that evaluation is very different, and all these changes can be very intimidating for teachers and students alike. Using portfolio evaluation makes different kinds of demands that both teachers and students must be willing to accept, but teachers must make the more drastic changes and commit to them first. Until teachers can explain why they are moving to portfolio evaluation, until they can explain how they see portfolio evaluation supporting the curriculum, and until they can outline clearly for students (and colleagues, if need be) how portfolio evaluation will work, they shouldn't consider implementing it.

But portfolios also represent a new understanding of evaluation of student efforts and even programmatic assessment. More and more professional educators are recognizing that writing in particular cannot be evaluated by means of testing or even by grading one-shot writing situations. I am certain we will see portfolio evaluation used by more teachers and programs in the future.

CHAPTER 2

WHY USE PORTFOLIOS?

This is by no means an easy question to answer. However, if you are willing to look at education and your role as a teacher from some different perspectives, you might find that portfolios fit your personality and reflect your beliefs better than you think.

FIRST, IT'S A MATTER OF WHAT YOU BELIEVE IS IMPORTANT

I can't speak for everyone who uses portfolios in the classroom, but I suspect the assertions I make here are representative of the beliefs of a good portion. Teachers who use portfolios tend to have a different perspective on education in general:

- ❑ Teaching does not involve the dissemination of knowledge by an expert; instead, students learn by solving problems, by honing critical thinking skills, and by practicing.

- ❑ Teachers are expert resources who serve as guides or coaches in the learning processes of their students.

While many teachers of many disciplines might agree with these statements, the composition teacher who makes these assertions reveals much about her philosophy of composition instruction. She

15

identifies herself with the tenets and practices of modern composition theory. That is, she believes

- that learning to write involves experimenting and developing a process, not exclusive attention to a product;

- that every rhetorical situation is different, demanding different kinds of thinking, tools, skills, and guidance;

- that problem solving within a specific rhetorical situation is more valuable than direct instruction of a specific tool (or mode; besides, aren't all essays developed using several tools in support of each other? I can't imagine a comparison/contrast essay without description, and I can't imagine a writer determining the tools to use before discovering his or her purpose for writing);

- that working within real-world situations (or as real as they can be in an institutional setting) are more instructional than completing traditional formulas (the five-paragraph essay, for example, which doesn't even exist in the real world);

- that students must to be able to experiment without the threat of failure;

- that not all students need exactly the same practice and guidance in exactly the same areas or with the same tools;

- that students need time and the opportunity to develop their own voices and style;

- that students learn to write by writing;

- that in addition to learning to communicate, writing promotes learning in other areas (particularly about the self);

- that, ultimately, what the student learns about writing is of more importance than the letter grade he or she gets at the end.

This last point is the one that prevents some teachers from ever using portfolios. They are often too afraid of the backlash from students (and parents) who hold the grade in higher regard. But teachers who are more concerned with providing students with solid opportunities to learn realize they have to develop a thick skin to withstand that backlash and do so willingly. That doesn't mean they aren't hurt by or affected by the negative reactions to portfolios, but it does mean they realize the constant need to reaffirm what they believe is important in their teaching.

Teachers who hold these certain beliefs about education and what teaching means tend to use different pedagogies, too:

- Assignments that present a problem to be solved, usually by the definition of the rhetorical situations or goals to be met, not a specific text (mode) to achieve (see Sample 2.1, p. 18);

- Various kinds of prewriting opportunities - including talking, reading, and writing - that allow the student to tackle the problem presented (see Sample 2.2. p. 19);

- Peer and teacher responses to drafts in progress, available over the course of the term;

Sample # 2.1: Assigning by rhetorical situation, not mode

ENGL 0110 / Fall 1999 / Essay 2
An expository essay based on observations

What is in the world and what can it teach us? What do we see if we really watch and pay attention? What does what we see mean to us? And can it mean more to others?

What does what is out there mean?

The final draft of this essay will explain something about the world you come to know through analysis of observations of something, some one, some place and the activities that occur in it. People might be the focus, but something else might catch your attention, too.

This essay will discuss, explain, and argue for the results of your thinking about several different things – your observations, your analysis of those observations, and your study of metaphor.

Purpose of Assignment: to practice observation, to analyze observations

Purpose of Paper: to share analysis and to argue for your conclusions about observation with readers, making a point about some aspect of the world.

Audience: Others who might have seen the same thing but who have not analyzed it

Voice: First person is appropriate

Style: Semi-formal

Special Considerations: No 5-paragraph essays, please; be sure to SHOW us what you saw, not just TELL us.

Sample # 2.2: Prewriting suggestions that accompany assignment

Prewriting Suggestions for Essay 2: Observation Essay

Today in class: discuss possible sites for observations with your group members; discuss specific audience related to each site identified.

Suggestion 1: From the list of places you identified with your group members, select one; describe it in as much detail as you can (in a journal entry or a freewrite or a list).

Then, go to that site; take your description with you and observe: How accurate is your description? What did you leave out of your description? What did you mis-remember? Add to your description and delete erroneous details.

What kinds of details did you leave out? What do they have in common? What does that tell you about how you view the world?

Suggestion 2: Pick on of the sites your peer group identified as a good place to observe and LIST as many predictions as you can: What do you expect to see?

Then, go to that site; take your predictions with you and observe: How accurate are your predictions? What did you see that is surprising to you?

Why do you think you didn't predict them? What do they have in common? What does that tell you about how you view the world?

If you don't like what you saw, if you didn't SEE anything, where else could you go to conduct your observation?

- Lots of revising opportunities and specific instruction for revising certain weak features, using the students' own texts as samples (with their permissions, of course)

- Publication in some fashion (the portfolio, even though I am the only one able to enjoy it)

The teachers who commit to these pedagogies are not the teachers who spend time doing skill-and-drill exercises out of handbooks, either. Instead, the handbook becomes the basis for lots of short, focused lessons (mini-lessons; see Chapter 1) that focus on weak examples from the students' papers; class time is devoted to analyzing the weaknesses or grammatical error in student samples, discussing ways to improve the weakness or resolve the grammatical error, and time for students to look for and mark weaknesses or error in their own papers for later attention. In other words, these teachers know that learning happens best within the context of what the students are doing.

> **PS**
>
> Samples from student papers, either current or former, work much better than handbook exercises. Just remember to get the students' permissions to use their work first! I usually send around a sheet for them to sign, indicating whether they want me to use their material or not.

Teachers who use portfolio evaluation tend to have a different perspective on evaluating the writing they ask their students to do, too. Most believe that

- continual improvement over the course of a term is a myth;

- students can change their basic writing ability with continual practice;

- no one piece can adequately represent a writer's ability;

- not all students have the same strengths and weaknesses or even the ability to recognize and address them;

- writing ability cannot be quantified, but it can be described;

- writing ability is more than a matter of being able to apply rules of grammar and mechanics correctly;

- writing is not a competition sport; writers shouldn't be evaluated on a comparison basis.

In case you haven't guessed by now, all these statements are true of me, and they are the ideas I explain to students when I introduce them to portfolio evaluation.

HOW STUDENTS REACT TO PORTFOLIO EVALUATION

Though skeptical at first, many students soon realize that portfolios will allow them the time they need to develop good essays, that they will receive lots of support from me (if and when they ask for it), and that they aren't working alone on the tasks I assign. On course evaluations, some even comment that they appreciated the fact that the portfolio method let them work on papers as much as they wanted or needed to and at their own pace.

But yes, you're right if you are thinking that some students don't like portfolios at all. Portfolios demand too much that is foreign to them. Portfolios demand that students

- accept ownership of their own work;

- take responsibility for fulfilling requirements;

❑ reflect and self-evaluate;

❑ keep track of everything.

> **PS**
>
> Two things: every piece of writing should have a name ("journal" or "freewrite") and numbering them helps. Dating each piece will also help you and students keep track of what is done.

And, students have to look at writing differently. Portfolios ask them to see writing not as a challenge to determine "what the teacher wants" and to achieve some ideal text. Instead, writing has to be something they must

❑ invest themselves in,

❑ see as valuable and important,

❑ see as worthy of their time and effort for something other than a grade.

In other words, writing must become something students think about without worrying about correctness or the final grade. That's hard for the many who claim grades are their principle motivation ("I have to know how I'm doing in relation to the rest of the class.") or their only real concern ("I have to have an A to get into med school!"). Those are the students who have the hardest time with portfolio evaluation.

For the students who *can* put the almighty grade aside and focus on learning, portfolios become something that allows them to

❑ work at their own pace;

❑ receive response when they need it;

❑ work within a community of other writers;

22

- learn from other writers;

- improve weaknesses;

- see connections between papers/situations and apply newly learned or developed skills to each;

- revise as much as they feel they need or want to;

- put a text away to revise after time has allowed them a more objective view of their strengths and weaknesses.

SELF-EVALUATION VS. TEACHER EVALUATION

This last point, time to let the paper age, contributes to another important aspect portfolios encourage, self-evaluation. Maybe the most important benefit of portfolio evaluation is the shared responsibility for evaluation that it demands from teachers and students.

For students to be able to accept ownership and so much responsibility for their own decisions, teachers need to give up some authority in one other area: evaluation. If students feel they have some say in the evaluation process, they are much more likely to take their work seriously and to work to understand the requirements of them. However, students must know that the teacher is sincere in her insistence that students do have something important to say about their own work; that is, teachers must be willing to try to see the quality of the writing the student claims he or she sees.

23

To self-evaluate means that first, students must have the benefit we claim as writers to step back and look at our work through readers' eyes. The time that students need to achieve this distance (which is much longer than you or I might need) is provided only by the portfolio evaluation system. After two weeks of not even looking at a paper, students will be able to spot weakness, examples of weaknesses or errors from recent mini-lesson instruction, and have the time to revise to improve. All the time offered here allows, even forces, students to accept the responsibility for their own work. They can think more, reflect more, read more, and even revise more, all processes that mean they have to take their own work more seriously than usual.

Second, students need to be part of our evaluation process; the teacher needs to hear about strengths each writer sees in his or her own work, the weaknesses and problems they encountered and how each tried to address them, and even an over all sense of what changes in writing each student has observed. Why? Often, in examining their work from this perspective, students will reveal something about themselves as writers or even their processes that will help us understand why a certain error or weakness continues to surface, even after we have addressed it in mini-lessons. Because we are treating them as real writers, students need what real writers need, to have the chance to take a breather and reflect on what they have done, both as they work on revisions and as they approach completion of each paper, or, more formally (as it is in my class) at mid-term (see Chapter 4).

SOME DISADVANTAGES
OF USING PORTFOLIO EVALUATION

Don't some students resist the idea of self-evaluation? Yes, but the teacher can explain the reasons for using portfolios yet again (I have yet to have a class where *every* student gets every point I make the first time I make it; why should portfolios be any different?). And, don't some students still fail because they put the work off until the last minute? Yes, but they know (or can be reminded that they should know) exactly why they failed, and they can't blame anyone but themselves for it. They realize that they let themselves down by not recognizing one of the biggest problems any writer (but especially college freshmen) will face in using the portfolio method: Procrastination! If they don't keep up with the work, if they don't work daily on their papers, if they wait until the night before to finish three or four papers, they cannot do their best work, and they have cheated themselves out of opportunities to learn through peer responses and my help on revisions.

> ## *PS*
> I experimented one quarter: I asked students to keep a process log, a daily record of what they worked on, how long they spent on it, and what exactly they did. The log was due weekly. It worked, to a certain extent, but I gave it up; it just became one other piece of paper for them and me to keep track of. But it did seem to help the procrastinators by illustrating just how much time they were losing!

Some students will always wait until the last minute to do any writing, whether it be drafting or revising, but I bet you'll hear "I work better under pressure" no matter what grading protocol you use. I've even had students come late to the final exam because they were still working on final drafts of their papers.

One of the biggest drawbacks to portfolios

Deciding who is responsible for the student completing work is the one aspect of portfolio evaluation that still gives me trouble. On one hand, I don't want to be the one responsible for making them do the work; I don't want to be Big Brother, watching over their shoulders. On the other hand, I know that freshman in particular are so distracted by every other aspect of college life that they need a major jolt to help them establish some priorities.

So, I find I can't totally give up my sense of responsibility to them, either; I have had to find some compromises. I still have to play a role I don't relish; I still have to play policeman, making sure they have completed whatever assignment I have made. That's why there are specific due dates for specific drafts and why I hint about visiting during office hours, especially after mid-term when their homework consists mainly of working on revisions of early papers.

So what happens when a student does procrastinate and shows up without a draft on the day assigned? Does he get a zero? No; no numbers, remember? But the fact that he didn't have the draft that day is something I record (see Chapter 3) and can bring up later if he is not happy with the final grade he gets on his portfolio. And, he still must fulfill the responsibility of being a good peer responder; he just doesn't reap the same benefits as everyone else does. And, if he does want response to a draft later on, he must negotiate with his peers, something most students will be quite reluctant to do. Students won't learn if we don't give them the chance to; I choose to give up the responsibility for them completing their work for the simple fact that it is not mine, and they have to have the chance to learn that. My only responsibilities in this situation are to make clear that something is due and to provide adequate time for the student to complete the task.

Not all teachers are comfortable giving up this amount of responsibility; they feel they have to be able to provide proof to justify whatever grade they eventually submit for any student. For that reason, they use grades as a system of punishment rather than a reflection of writing ability. I understand that reluctance, but I also know that using grades to punish doesn't achieve anything, expect maybe apathy, distrust, and frustration all around. And none of these describe the educational environment I (or most students) want to be a part of.

Teachers who use portfolios have realized that they must commit to something other than making sure they can justify the grade they ultimately assign. In a way, they have agreed to become a teacher of life's lessons as well as of writing. I know that if I gave that student the opportunity to do something, and he didn't take it, that I am not responsible for what he does not do. And, I know that by not taking advantage of that opportunity, the student has probably hurt his chances of doing his best work; I just hope he eventually realizes that somehow, too (and most do, whether they admit it to me or not). In a contrary sense, I suppose, I have to accept a different responsibility and take the opportunity to teach that student another kind of lesson, one that I think is part of being a college student. Isn't learning to be responsible for your own actions part of growing up and being successful in college and the real world? A boss might even go so far as to fire an employee for not fulfilling his responsibilities, right? Once I remind the student of this truth, once I remind him that I don't *give* grades, that students *earn* grades, I have met my responsibility. I have offered as many opportunities for him to learn as I possibly can.

This attitude might seem harsh, but rarely do I encounter a student who has yet to figure out that taking advantage of opportunities is part of real life. I've had more students admit that they could have done B-level writing but that their portfolios deserve a C because they didn't do all they could have than I have had students who cannot accept the responsibility for their own education.

Do I reach every student? No. How do I know? They say so, sometimes in mean and vindictive comments on course evaluations. Am I affected by these comments? Yes and no. Yes, because I am a human being who can be hurt by vicious, negative reactions (and we all get them). But no, because I know that I have offered the same opportunities to all, that I have managed to affect some positive change in some students along the way, and that I have been part of their learning, and I have been as objective as possible in my evaluation. I know those students will be better prepared for life. They are the ones who keep me teaching and reinforce my dedication to portfolio evaluation. These benefits for me as the teacher far outweigh the disadvantages.

HOW EXACTLY DOES THE TEACHER BENEFIT FROM USING PORTFOLIOS?

The biggest benefit for me is that I can be the kind of teacher I know I want and need to be: the experienced guide.

Portfolios allow me the luxury

- ❏ to be a real reader and responder to student writing,

- ❏ to evaluate when it is appropriate (at the end, when the writer declares a piece finished),

- ❏ to follow development of skills on an individual basis,

- ❏ to figure out which of my instructions made sense and which only confused them,

- to address individual learning styles,

- to keep track of what students are doing (or not doing),

- to observe their processes and their decision making schema,

- to individualize instruction.

Individualized instruction is probably the single most important benefit for me; being able to work one-on-one allows me to address specific needs and concerns I know each student has. I can earn their trust, participate in their processes when I need to, and teach specific concepts when they are needed, not just when they occur in the syllabus. I can allow weaker writers time to work out problems without holding back the stronger writers. I can, in a word, teach.

> **PS**
>
> This individualized instruction happens mostly in conferences; I can cover specific mechanical and grammatical issues then and not have to bore the whole class. And, I have the student's paper to show him or her exactly what I mean. I'll show him or her how to fix the first instance, and then mark the rest with only a check mark in the margin.

There are two other benefits that both allow me to do something else I find valuable: I get to work from the positive. I'm not constantly telling students something is wrong or inappropriate; in fact, I have more opportunities to show them what they do well and why.

29

Writing to develop fluency

One aspect of teaching that portfolios allow me to I indulge in is assigning short, practice pieces as homework. No, these aren't busy work; they have a real, pedagogical basis that I discuss with students.

Instead of giving the traditional quiz over the reading assignment, I assign freewrite responses (FWRs) to essays they read. These are one-typed page (that's the challenge, anyway) of thinking-on-paper; that is, I ask students to respond to the idea(s) they read. These FWRs are not summaries or explications; they are to be thoughtful reactions to another writer's ideas (see Sample 2.3 below for some suggestions I make when I first assign FWRs). These assignments are my way of offering writing-to-learn experiences to my students. I am always astounded by the number of students who tell me that these become the most valuable kind of writing they do because it makes them think.

Sample 2.3: FWR starter suggestions

FWRs are just that – **responses** – not interpretations, criticisms, analyses. **THINK** about what you just read. **Explore** and **explain** and **record** as many of your thoughts/ideas/events/experiences that this piece reminded you of. Try one of these if you get stuck:

1. I began to think of . . .
2. I was surprised/I wonder . . .
3. I really don't/can't understand . . .
4. I know the feeling of . . .
5. I thought/think /noticed. . .
6. I can't believe . . .
7. I like the way . . .
8. If I had been/I suppose that . . .
9. The part about X reminds me of /connects to. . .
10. I suspect Dr. Mc wanted us to read this because . . .

And, because I respond to the FWRs as if I were participating in a dialectical journal situation (that is, I talk to them through my comments instead of grading them), students have more opportunities to see how a reader responds to their writing and why. Even better for me is the fact that I can work from the positive. I can point out some nicely phrased idea or one that grabs my attention. And if they say something funny, I can laugh!

What specifically do I mark and respond to? Here's another luxury: I can be a real reader. I can respond to whatever delights me, causes a reaction in me, confuses me, or challenges me. I've had to develop some new marks (see Sample 2.4, p. 32); I use symbols that reflect questions, reactions, and emotions (freshmen assure me that smiley faces are not too juvenile for them; however, I do have to make sure they know I mean "I'm smiling" not "This is correct/good."), or I ask questions, especially questions about why they believe some idea or how some idea is a truth for them.

> **PS**
> Actually, these are symbols I use in responding to drafts, mostly; some of them are not appropriate for the purposes of the FWRs. I don't tend to worry about transitions in FWRs, for instance.

How do FWRs develop fluency? By giving them honest, real-reader feedback, I am showing the students where in their texts I need more help in understanding their thinking. Inevitably, they challenge themselves to add enough information to prevent me from having to ask a question. They tell me they know they are doing well when they don't get a paper back with "why?" on it, and they are usually right! They figure out (usually by midterm) that all the practice they are doing in the FWRs makes writing the papers easier. They tell me they like to see that I ask far fewer questions on later FWRs; they call this "improvement," and I don't disagree (even though I consider it more being conscious of how readers respond; that in itself is an improvement worth noting).

Sample 2.4: Symbols for responding to FWRs and drafts

These are ones I use constantly – for every writing situation. Feedback I get tells me that once I explain them, the students like them because they know where to look for places to revise.

⫽	Movement between paragraphs is missing; I'm not prepared for this idea yet
Ⓣ	Wait – the sentence before this mark doesn't seem to have anything to do with the sentence after it – no flow of ideas or connections for me as reader
_?!	Wait – I don't understand the phrase/sentence (usually in [ ] in text. Could you maybe say it a different way? I had to read it 3 times to get it!
〰〰	Under a portion of text –this means something sounds funny to me here – want to check diction level and word choice? Maybe there is a clearer/more appropriate way to say it for the audience?
‿	This made me laugh or happy
⌃	This made me sad or feel sorry for you
‿‿‿	This means, yeah I know, ewwwwww!
_huh?	Huh? I just don't get this; can you say it differently?
weary? weary	I'm confused; do you maybe mean this word instead?
ⓘt ?	But what's "it?" I don't know and I'm confused.
X (,) xx xxx	you might want to check on this comma; it threw me off.

Most students tell me this kind of writing is by far most beneficial over all for another reason: They get to say what they think without having to worry about grammar, error, spelling, etc. Learning to think on papers and interpret my responses on the FWRs is the first challenge we meet; the second involves that intimidating (or so they tell me) one-on-one meeting in my office.

Conferences are a vital component of portfolio evaluation

Our departmental guidelines suggest holding a conference with each student three times a quarter; I require one on each major paper they are assigned as well as a mid-term conference. Sometimes that means as many as four conferences over the course of ten weeks. And, since I no longer punish myself by writing lengthy comments on student papers, I have no problem giving up class time, office hours, and even some free time for these conferences. Besides, I have learned that I can get more direct instruction and negotiation of a text accomplished in a fifteen-minute conference than I can in writing comments. Quality interaction with the writer, being able to see whether or not he or she understands my concerns, occurs best in the conference.

Many who write about teaching writing will suggest that students know best when they need response, and that we should not force them to come see us in mandatory conferences. In theory, I agree, But practical experience has taught me that freshmen will not come to discuss their work on a volunteer basis, that few are ever aware that they are ready for response. Why? Some will procrastinate, putting off revisions until the last possible moment. Or, they are just too afraid (or so they tell me) to come to office hours. So, I require conferences, and I start early in the term. In the first required one, we talk about the early draft of their first paper, the reactions and concerns they have to the class, and anything else that might come up. I try to make sure they leave that first conference feeling good about what they have been doing but with a clear understanding of what else they probably want to devote time to during the quarter.

You might think students resent taking time for these conferences, but after the first one, they seem more willing to visit during office hours and to make appointments for the rest of the required conferences. They tell me later on that they appreciate (for the most part) the individual attention they get, not to mention the fact that they can be candid about their concerns. Comments on course evaluations invariably mention conferences as the means by which I was most effective in working with students.

Conferences serve as a way for us to negotiate peer responses and suggestions and for me to add some additional suggestions as students venture into serious revision tasks. As the term goes on, they can ask for a conference on a revision any time they are ready for it. All I ask in return is overnight to read the paper and some information on what they want response to. I continue to require conferences on each of the major papers assigned, but by the last such conference, and even conferences on later drafts of earlier assignments, I insist that the student conduct it. That is, the student has to tell me what he or she knows is (still) weak in the paper, how he or she intends to address that weakness, and what other revisions the paper might need. Only then will I add my comments, observations, and

> **PS**
>
> I do have one firm rule: Only one paper at a time. Otherwise, they'll wait until the last minute and try to have me read everything at once. But this means we have to do a how-many-conference-opportunities-left countdown to the last day of office hours.

suggestions. Does this work? Can students conduct conferences by the end of the term? Amazingly enough, yes. When I tell them to be prepared, they are. If they aren't, well, we don't have much to talk about, do we? That is their choice; I must respect it.

A QUICK SUMMARY

I've shared lots of information in this chapter and left you with quite a bit to think about. Let me try to sum up the main points before I move on to other aspects of portfolio evaluation you will want to consider.

Overall, what are the advantages of portfolio evaluation?

- ✓ The student becomes responsible for his or her own work and for keeping track of it.

- ✓ Record keeping is easily done in a record book and is simpler; there is no math to do at the end of the term.

- ✓ The final grade is more representative of the student's writing ability.

- ✓ The final grade is more objective since it reflects the totality of the work, not an average of individual pieces.

- ✓ At any given time, teachers will have to be only responders; that is, they won't have to split their attention between grading one set of papers and responding to another.

And the disadvantages?

I wouldn't be honest if I said there weren't any, and I have mentioned several. Students' negative reactions aside, I think you'll want to remember the following points especially; they are the ones that have given me the most trouble over the years.

- ✓ Lots of reading at the end of the term; all the final drafts must be read holistically. Review of other material is necessary, too. But, there is no need for response; the papers are complete.

- ✓ Quality of the final papers is sometimes disappointing, especially if the decision of what to submit is left up to the student. Negotiating the definition of good writing is critical.

- ✓ Deadlines and procrastination: Some students just can't handle the responsibilities portfolios ask of them. And some students refuse to; they will maintain that the responsibility for making sure something gets done belongs to the teacher.

- ✓ The inevitable quandary: Do we grade quality or quantity? Is the grade of C for a portfolio fair to the student who has worked consciously over the course of the term and truly done his or her best? (More on this in Chapter 4.)

And, experience has taught me that college teachers who use portfolios have to have a much thicker skin; many freshman today firmly believe that my responsibility is to tell them exactly what to do and how to do it so they can have the grade they "need." When I can't and don't agree, they blame the portfolio system.

There are some other issues that some teachers might consider disadvantages, too.

Managing the Work Load

This aspect of portfolios isn't really that much different; I still have FWRs, in-class journal writing, and papers to read and respond to. But I find that I can spread these out over the term more and not have something to read every single night of the week. The major work for me comes at mid-term when I must review and evaluate the portfolio prior to a conference and at the end of the

PS

And, I get a break on the days drafts are due: no FWRs to read. Maybe there is a journal I want to look over, but that takes 20 minutes before class and is a good way to prepare and remind myself about issues we need to discuss.

term when I am under pressure to get grades to the registrar.

For the mid-term conference, I've learned to give myself the weekend to prepare and to cancel class and schedule most of the conferences on the following Monday. When I prepare myself mentally for the task to come, I can read eighteen portfolios over a weekend and conduct eighteen conferences on Monday. I've found that I can retain most of the information I want to in short-term memory if I jot key words on a post-it note. However, some teachers might want to prepare a checklist, detailing goals and problems, to mark as they read each portfolio.

For the final portfolio reading and evaluating, I've learned to pace myself and take frequent breaks. When all I have to do is read, keeping the rubric in mind, evaluating a portfolio can take a little as twenty to thirty minutes. Yes, that's far longer than it takes to grade an objective test, but it is far less time than I would spend with a calculator figuring percentages, adding up totals, and finding averages.

Storage Concerns

One major problem for me is finding room in an already crowded office to keep the final portfolios, which I do for at least a year. Then I recycle the contents if the student hasn't picked it up (and I'm always disappointed by how many I have to recycle.). If your department requires that you keep student material on file for a year like mine does, you will probably have storage problems, too.

I've found that one file drawer in a standard file cabinet will hold between twenty and twenty-five portfolios (depending on how thick they are). But I always run out of drawer space, so plastic crates are also a feature of my office (I have three that I stack under the end of the computer table, out of the way.). The trick, I've discovered, is making sure each portfolio takes up as little space as possible. That's one reason I have the students turn in material in file folders rather than a binder; I ask them not to submit papers in plastic report covers, fancy plastic folders, etc. I just don't have the room.

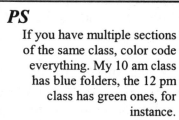

PS

If you have multiple sections of the same class, color code everything. My 10 am class has blue folders, the 12 pm class has green ones, for instance.

You might be fortunate enough to find storage space in a departmental storage room. Or, you can always keep a box in the corner of your garage or storage room at home.

38

ONE LAST PHILOSOPHICAL CONSIDERATION

Portfolio evaluation allows me to try to address one major problem facing higher education today, that of grade inflation. Far too many students who are competent writers are making grades that indicate an ability they don't have; that is, they can write at the C or B level most of the time, but because they are good at taking quizzes, they make an A in the course. That's the basic source of grade inflation, I think; students are being rewarded for hoop-jumping abilities instead of having writing abilities fairly evaluated. Many of us have encountered the student who has the I-must-make-an-88-on-this-quiz-if-I-want-an-A-in-this-course attitude; I have found that portfolio evaluation eliminates that thinking (even though I still hear the "I really have to make a B in this course!" comment more often that I really like to. "Go for it!" is my typical response, and it is a sincere one.).

Portfolio evaluation allows me to focus strictly on writing ability, not a student's ability to garner extra points. If the student is a C-level writer, he should receive a C in the course. Does this happen? Yes. I have actually had quarters in which no one has earned an A in my classes. Yet no one complained; each knew his or her own writing ability.

> **PS**
>
> I've learned to keep the rubric handy; the more I can refer to it, the more the students understand what they need to do to get the grade they want. And, I'll ballpark their grade at any time; that seems to help, too, especially if I ask them first to tell me how they think they are doing.

THE BOTTOM LINE

As a teacher of writing, I don't want to be someone who merely judges how well a student has jumped a hoop. And, I don't think writing is something to grade the way we do meat or diamonds. Student writing isn't that kind of commodity.

Instead, I want the grade for the course to provide some feedback on how well a student has applied the skills we discussed and he or she explored; I want to look at the overall completeness and competency evident in several pieces of writing; I want to evaluate how well the student has applied the principles and techniques we have discussed in class. And, I want to hear what that student thinks, too. I don't think I alone have the right to evaluate that student's work. But, we have to consider what to evaluate, first.

CHAPTER 3

WHAT GOES INTO PORTFOLIOS? AND HOW DO I INTRODUCE PORTFOLIO EVALUATION TO STUDENTS?

KINDS OF PORTFOLIOS

You'll see several different terms used to describe portfolios, depending on the grade level and discipline; *learning portfolios* are popular in elementary classrooms where teachers (and parents) want to see daily work. In junior and senior high schools, *project portfolios* for literature, writing, and science classes seem most predominant. For the college composition classroom, however, two specific kinds of portfolios in particular seem most appropriate. In each, literally everything a student produces over the course of a grading term goes into the portfolio; what actually gets evaluated is different.

The Comprehensive Portfolio

Program curricula or departmental requirements make the *comprehensive portfolio* harder to work with; teachers with the freedom to develop their own curriculum will have an easier time.

Basically, the comprehensive portfolio system works like this: The teacher makes several regular assignments, and whatever the student writes in response to that assignment is saved. During the course of the term, the teacher provides time for students to review the contents of the portfolio; the student chooses which pieces he or she wants to work on. At the end of the term, the student is responsible for selecting the pieces he or she is most proud of for evaluation (a system that is almost impossible to use on the quarter system and only a bit easier to accomplish on the semester system).

A variation on this system that seems to work better for college composition classes allows students to select (at mid-term, perhaps) which three of five (for example) drafted essays to revise and complete by the end of the term (again, much easier on the semester system than on the quarter system). In programs where only word or page counts are mandated, this option allows for much more negotiation

> **PS**
> Due dates are still possible and even critical; students must have drafts for peer review sessions. I collect a file copy on those days, partly to have a copy in case something happens, but also to give them the sense something really is due.

between the teacher and student, but also demands much more from the student (in terms of being responsible for choices).

Teachers who are able to use comprehensive portfolios find they must carefully and consciously

- ❑ define specific goals for the course;

- ❑ establish a minimum amount of work required to meet those goals;

- ❑ specify the purpose of each assignment;

- explain how it achieves the goals for the course;

- establish very clear evaluation criteria;

- be prepared to read and respond quite often;

- respect student decisions.

Students will need more opportunities to conference with each other and the teacher, and they will need guidance in making the best choices. They will also have to understand that they will be responsible for the results of those choices. But, most students can and should be responsible for their own work.

The Defined Portfolio

This is the version I use; the term is one I've coined to differentiate my version from others. Because of articulation agreements mandated by state law, our composition program requirements dictate most of the portfolio contents that I must evaluate; each student is required to write a certain number of and kinds of papers, the evaluation of which constitutes most of their final grade in the course (at least 80% for those who use traditional grading procedures). However, our program allows for several approaches and even the possibility of ungraded writing being assigned, so I have quite a bit of professional autonomy in designing assignments to achieve the goals of the course.

I, therefore, define the specific contents of the portfolio students must submit at midterm and the end of the term. The specific contents match the departmental requirements of number and kinds of papers, but I am free to require that all writing they do over the term is also included.

THE PHYSICAL ASPECTS
OF KEEPING THE PORTFOLIO

The major responsibility students must accept from the first day is to keep track of their work. I suggest a binder or file-folder system since there is lots of trading back and forth of loose paper. Being organized is a must; some students find this more than challenging. I suggest a special box or corner of their desk at home as the special place to put everything if they don't want to carry it in a notebook to class.

When I collect drafts and revisions to review for conferences, I provide a file folder; on it, students can write me notes or questions, I can jot information about problems and successes for us to discuss in conference. The file folder becomes a different kind of record keeping device for me; I can see what that student said about early drafts, etc.

The file folder becomes the portfolio, for all practical purposes. Students submit the contents of the final portfolio in it instead of some bulky binder. At least that is the system that works best for me.

Checklists

Even though I explain that students are to save everything, they rarely take me seriously or literally. I have found that at mid-term and at the end of the term, both, I need to provide students with a checklist of what specifically must be in the portfolio (see Sample 3.1, p. 45). I actually don't mind doing this; I find it serves as a reminder to me, too, of what I need to revisit before I determine a final grade.

Sample 3.1: Final portfolio contents checklist

ENGL 0112 – Winter 2000 - Final Portfolio Instructions

Final drafts of all papers are to be typed, proofed, and initialed; everything else should be in original state.

- ❏ *THIS SHEET /**SIGN** PERMISSION FORM **(ON BACK) – OPTIONAL***

*****I still have Short Paper 1; I will put it in your portfolio.*****

- ❏ **Essay 1 (magazine paper), final draft**
- ❏ **Short Paper 2 (memo), final draft** - including
  - ❏ References/Works Cited page
  - ❏ copy of sources
- ❏ **Essay 2, final draft** –including
  - ❏ References/Works Cited page
  - ❏ copy of sources
- ❏ **Essay 3, final draft** – including
  - ❏ References/Works Cited page
  - ❏ copy of sources
- ❏ **Short Paper 3 (annotated bib), final draft**
  - ❏ copy of rest of sources (not used in Essays 2 & 3)
- ❏ **Short Paper 4 (précis), final draft** – including
  - ❏ article it is based on

- ❏ **All** FWRs
- ❏ **All Journals**
- ❏ **All** prewriting, drafts, & peer responses for Essays 1 – 3 and Short Papers 2 – 4.

Your portfolio is due at the beginning of the exam period.

RECORD KEEPING ISSUES

One major change actually simplifies the day-to-day paper keeping tasks. If you look at Sample 3.2 below, you will notice how easy it is to record whether students do the work or not; all I use is a check mark to indicate that the assignment was submitted or an X to indicate that it was not. At the end of the quarter, I can easily and quickly see how much of the assigned work each student did. No numbers to add up and average; no percentages to calculate. The grade book becomes more of a record book, and I don't even have to use a book; I develop my own record sheets using the table function of my word processing program.

Sample 3.2: Example of my record page for FWRS

ENGL 0110 101 FWRS Fall 1999	1	2	3	4	5	6	Etc . . .
Brown, Bobby	✓	✓	X	✓			
Christianson, Joe	✓	✓	✓	X			
Davis, Peggy	✓-	✓-	✓-	✓			
Ethridge, Jane	✓	✓	✓	✓+			
Frank, Tom	✓	✓	✓	✓			
Jones, Celeste	X	X	X	X			
Etc . . .							
Due date	5/3	5/5	5/9	5/12			

INTRODUCING PORTFOLIO EVALUATION
TO STUDENTS

Especially if you are new to using portfolios, you will always find introducing and explaining the concept to students to be a major challenge. Some teachers I know will give their students the choice of using portfolio evaluation or the traditional grade-each-paper method; I have yet to hear of a class that voluntarily chooses portfolios.

I don't give my students a choice, I admit. But, on the first day of class, I do make sure I

- ❏ explain the process: what will and will not be evaluated and when evaluation will occur;

- ❏ explain why I use portfolio evaluation;

- ❏ provide a written description of how portfolio evaluation works in my class (see Sample 3.3, p. 48);

- ❏ provide a written description of the course requirements for the portfolio contents;

- ❏ provide a detailed grading rubric;

- ❏ explain that students will have a role in the evaluation of their work;

- ❏ promise that I will let them know as soon as their work falls below the C level as described on the rubric.

Sample #3.3: Portfolio description from policy statement

ENGL 0110 –FALL 1999 – GRADING POLICY

The ***portfolio method of evaluation*** that I use in this class is a fairly standard one for composition classes. It allows me to determine your overall writing ability, not your ability to jump hoops and "do what the teacher wants" on individual papers. As I described to you in class, portfolio evaluation works like this: nothing is graded throughout the quarter. Instead, we work together to develop a portfolio of your best work. You and I evaluate it twice – once at mid-term and once at the end of the quarter. This allows you multiple chances to produce your best work. I do not compare your work to others' in the class; I evaluate your abilities according to the description on a rubric (see later in this packet). Basically, your final grade reflects the **quality of the final papers** in your portfolio and the **quality of the work you produce on a daily basis**. All other factors constitute effort; evaluation of effort allows me a means of determining which way to go on a borderline grade. So, you will know how you're doing in the class – how hard are you working? What level of work are you producing on a consistent basis?

You will get a mid-term grade; you will have time to revise work to achieve a higher grade after mid-term. Remember that you may for a ball park grade at any time (I <u>will not</u>, however, grade individual pieces of work during the quarter). You will participate in the evaluation of your work; you will complete a mid-term self-evaluation and a final self-evaluation.

My assumptions about your efforts in this class:
I plan the course work on the assumption that you want an "A" in the course and that you want to learn something about improving your writing ability. I consider each assignment an opportunity for you to accomplish both goals. If you want to do well in the course, plan to spend at the least 1-2 hours a night (perhaps more!) preparing for class. (This is less than the assumed formula of 3-5 hours of preparation for every hour spent in class.) To learn to write well, you must work daily on it – especially if you want to learn/achieve a grade higher than a "C."

Please note:
Do not be misled by the term "creative" in the rubric. The writing for ENGL 0110 is academic and expository in nature. Just because a paper is "fine/OK/nothing wrong with it" doesn't mean it is an "A." My job is not to "tell you what to do to make an 'A.'" Neither does effort guarantee you a grade of "A." I expect you to work hard; I don't reward you for doing the work I assign/expect you to do.

But even this is not enough. In addition to explaining why I use portfolios in my introductory remarks, I write them a letter, explaining in more detail how I see my role as their teacher (see Sample 3.4, below). Their first homework assignment is to read the written explanation in the syllabus and my letter and to write a letter to me in response.

Sample 3.4: My letter to students

Dear ENGL 0112 students,

I want to make sure you understand why I use portfolio evaluation, and I want to make sure you have the chance to ask about it and share any concerns you have about it. So, please read the material I gave you in class plus this note before you write me one in response.

Here's where I'm coming from: I can't teach you to write. Why? Because, unlike what you may have been told or experienced in the past, there in no <u>one</u> way to do it <u>correctly</u>. Five paragraph formula essays are fine for some situations, but not all! Writing well depends on many factors – and that's what I want to teach you. So, I can – and do – provide opportunities for you to learn instead. And I use portfolio evaluation because I believe you need to learn to write in an environment that allows you to have <u>every</u> opportunity you need to be successful. That is, I believe you need time to work out problems you have. And, you need to have the chance to talk with me as often as you need to.

But portfolios won't work if 1) you don't accept the responsibility for your own education; 2) you insist on "figuring out what the teacher wants" and basing all your choices on that; 3) if you procrastinate.

Items 2 and 3 are my biggest concern because they cause us the most problems. So let me try to address them here: What I "want" is good writing – writing that has a point, has lots of examples and evidence, and that is clear and error-free. I assure you: there is no set, specific, ideal paper in my head that you have to guess at; there are no tricks. But this makes writing tougher for you, doesn't it? You have to make choices and see if they work. Don't worry, I'll help you make them and I'll let you know whether they work or not.

(con.)

49

Sample 3.4: My letter to students (con.)

Item 3 – procrastination – is the biggest fear I have. Contrary to what you might think, there are specific due dates for papers in this class. If you don't have the draft or revision at the time it is due, if it isn't as solid as you can make it by that point, you are the only one hurt. Why? Because you cheat yourself out of the chance to get help, not only from me but from your peers, too. Last quarter, several students blew off doing the drafting and revising; when it was due, peer response groups and conferences with me were pretty much a waste of time. And, their grades reflected this: Most only scraped by with a C. That saddened me; most were good writers. But they were lazy, and they blamed me and portfolios for their poor performance. Please: Don't Procrastinate! Yes, you have all quarter long to work on the portfolio, but waiting until the last minute to do the work will hurt your chance to learn something more about writing and even your grade.

Ok – there's a bit more about where I'm coming from. What concerns and questions do you have? Please be honest! I can't promise I'll be able to explain everything or to convince you, but I will answer your questions and address your concerns to the best of my ability.

KMC

I also invite those students who have major reservations about portfolio evaluation to discuss their concerns with me, and I even recommend that they drop the class if they don't think they can work within the portfolio system (this rarely ever happens, mainly because getting into our composition classes is so difficult).

One GTA I know, Angela Insenga, has developed her introduction of portfolios based on mine, but she has added something that teachers new to portfolios might find useful. She includes in her syllabus a list of terms that they must know and a contract (see Sample 3.5, p. 51); students are asked to sign it after they have read the course policy handout and had the chance to ask questions. She gives them at least three days to read, think about, and discuss their concerns with her. GTAs and other teachers new to portfolio evaluation might find a similar document useful, especially if they anticipate negative student reaction.

Sample 3.5: Angela's keyword checklist and contract

ENGL 0110
Insenga

Here's a checklist of key words you'll need to familiarize yourself with:

Effort   Portfolio Grading
Expository   Conferences
Rubric   Freewrites
Plagiarism   "FA"
"Innovative"   Responding
"Creative"   Evaluating
Formulaic   Peer Review
The English Center

~~~~~~~~~~~~~~~~~~~~~~~~~~~
ENGL 0110
Insenga
Contract

Your contract with me:

I have read the policy statement and do understand the responsibilities required of me in Ms. Insenga's ENGL 0110 class. I understand the portfolio grading method and have read the checklist, the rubric, and the rules set down in the policy statement. I enter into the class knowing how it will function, and how I must function within it.

_____
Student, Spring 1999, ENGL 0110

My contract with you:

I will act according to the policies discussed in the policy statement, and I will adhere to the checklist of my responsibilities as an instructor of ENGL 0110.

_____
Angela Insenga

The trick to presenting portfolios as a positive challenge, I think, is to be open and honest about the whys and hows of portfolio evaluation from day one. I introduce the concept, focus on the benefits portfolios allow students to have, stress the need for them to be responsible, and show them how the rubric reflects the departmental paper grading rubric. I make it a point to explain why I use portfolios, too, so students will know I am not playing some game designed to trick them. Students often tell me that my opening day comments are intimidating; this is, thank goodness, after they have discovered the opportunities portfolios affords them. I assure them I don't mean to be intimidating, but I do feel I owe them complete honesty from the beginning.

THE BOTTOM LINE

The decision of what to include in a portfolio is, ultimately, up to the individual instructor. However, programmatic requirements and even student feedback may influence that decision. I have never had trouble matching my defined portfolio method to the requirements of program I am teaching in, even though I have encountered some vastly diverse programs and requirements. Essentially, I want to have the chance to re-see everything the student has done; that helps me evaluate basic writing ability for that student. And introducing portfolio evaluation to students will set the tone for the course; I think we need to be positive and honest, focus on the benefits, and stress the role we are inviting the student to play in his or her own education.

CHAPTER 4

EVALUATING PORTFOLIOS

Notice that this chapter focuses on *evaluating* portfolios, not *grading* portfolios. There's a reason for that. I've come to decide that grading, evaluating, and assessing aren't the same thing, even though we often hear and use these terms interchangeably. I define each differently.

Grading is judging the merit worth of something, usually by comparing it to something else. It is task or product specific; the grade reflects the presence of certain unique characteristics or requirements. Diamonds are graded according to color and quality, and meat is graded according to standards set by the FDA, but is that the same kind of grading teachers do? We should grade according to a set of standards, but what I have observed is that some teachers determine a grade by comparing papers to each other. That seems dangerous and inherently unfair to me. Those grades tend to be far too subjective for an activity that needs to be as objective as possible.

> **PS**
>
> A student once confessed to me, "The grade has become a kind of scholarly god to whom I pay homage because it somehow says yes or no when teachers are unwilling to give personal encouragement." A rather sad commentary on our actions, I think.

I've always been bothered by that approach to grading. I don't want to see one student's efforts compared to another's; I didn't want that to happen to me when I was a student, so why would I want to do it as a teacher?

And, I've never been sure that writing can be quantified as neatly as some teachers insist it can be. What exactly does a grade of 78 mean? I know teachers who insist they can tell the difference between a paper that deserves an 85 and one that deserves an 86. They insist that the evidence is there, that it has to do with surface error or the number of examples, but when pressed, they can never explain specifics to me, let alone show me the evidence of 86-ness in the text. "I just feel it; the right number just comes to me," one teacher explained to me, and I couldn't help but cringe as I thought about those psychics we see on television who claim the same kind of ability. I wouldn't accept that teachers had that ability when I was a student; why should I claim to have it now? I don't want to, that's the whole point. I want to be able to explain to students what they do well and what hinders my understanding of a text. I don't think an 84 on a paper can do that.

> **PS**
>
> I happened to overhear two students discussing a grade on a paper one day; one woman was very angry about her grade of 84. But what made the situation worse was that apparently, the teacher had whited-out one grade and written in another. The student was able to scratch off the white-out and discover the original grade was an 85. Just what made that teacher change that grade by one point?

And what about the teachers who deduct points for errors? If I deduct points for misspelled words, doesn't that tell the student I'm more concerned with spelling than I am with the message he or she is trying to communicate to me? I think this approach perpetuates the top-down attitude toward evaluation. Instead of recognizing the basic strength of a paper and the characteristics that mark it better than what we expect students to be able to do, deducting points seems to say that the paper was great, but because of these flaws, it deserves to be punished.

And, none of these ideas identify how a grade for a course should be determined, what the grade should be based on, or even what the grade should reflect. Ideally, I wouldn't grade papers in a composition course at all; I think many of us would be perfectly happy with a Pass/Fail system of evaluating writing ability. But teachers have to issue a grade; we know that. Grades are the paycheck that students work for, they are the evidence we offer the university that students have been successful, and grades are often important in opportunities for jobs or other pursuits students have after they leave our classes.

However, I believe that as a writing teacher, I have to focus on the aspects of writing that I know are important, namely the goals of the course, the purpose of the course within the departmental goals, and even the overall meaning of a college degree. I know I need to be concerned with grammatical and mechanical correctness, but I don't want to focus on some arbitrary rightness or even how much better one piece of writing is than another.

Instead, I want to look at the degree of success I have as a reader: Did I get the point? How well do I understand it? That's why I'd rather *evaluate* overall writing ability than grade individual instances of it. For me, *evaluation is a considered response, by an experienced (and demanding) reader, to the degree of success I have relative to the goals the writer set me up to expect.*

That is, how successful am I in seeing what the text tells me I will see? Or, to see writing ability from the writer's perspective, how successful was he or she at communicating to the reader? This success can and does vary from paper to paper, but good teachers can, I think, determine an overall level of success from evaluating a body of work. I must use my experience with students, with texts, with reading to evaluate the effectiveness of texts.

This kind of response demands that I have a benchmark, a standard to start from. Responsible writing teachers have traditionally used the rubric or general description to identify characteristics of a grade (much the same way an expert will use specific criteria to grade a diamond), but that's not appropriate for what I want to do. I need to see evidence of ability throughout all the papers the students have written; I want to evaluate their ability within the context of the course goals, not by how well they can write a specific kind of paper.

On one level, *assessment* is more what I think portfolios allow us to do: We can define the level of writing ability we see demonstrated across several samples of a writer's work if we evaluate that work using accepted descriptors of criteria. We can see the effort that went into achieving that work as well (if we take up drafts, responses, revisions, etc., which I do). In other words, our evaluation of ability is based on cumulative results, not on some arbitrary benchmark that gives us a number that gets added to another and another.

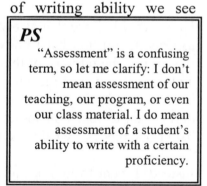

PS

"Assessment" is a confusing term, so let me clarify: I don't mean assessment of our teaching, our program, or even our class material. I do mean assessment of a student's ability to write with a certain proficiency.

IMPORTANCE OF A RUBRIC

Expecting students to write within a vacuum isn't fair, either; they have a right to know what criteria of evaluation that I use. Too many teachers I know grade without any kind of criteria or rubric guiding their decision. That's the most problematic (not to mention unfair and dangerous) kind of education I can imagine; it is exceptionally biased and arbitrary. Students have no chance of learning if all they do is fulfill someone's idiosyncratic ideas of what a particular paper should look like. But teachers who use a departmental or programmatic rubric to grade individual papers fall prey to a similar kind of problem. Fulfilling the criteria of the rubric becomes the goal students focus on: "What do I have to do to this paper to make it an A?" The writing to the rubric becomes the goal; the goal of the course, the purpose of needing to learn to write, the importance of writing within the university and life all become secondary if they are recognized at all. And, the teacher often finds herself in the position of having to defend a grade, especially if the rubric does not provide a clear picture of the relative importance of the characteristics named.

When all these concerns are put aside, when the focus of the class becomes the overall writing ability and not the rubric, learning happens. It may not happen to all students the same way and in the same degree, but it happens. If I can talk to students about revision options, if I can challenge them to revise for sentence clarity after they have organized the material in a logical manner, if I can get them to read for the little things that make writing really good (the fun stuff for us: parallelism and active verbs) I've helped them learn something. But I can't do all of that at once. We have to have time, and portfolios allow us to take that time.

But evaluation, reflected in the form of a letter grade, is still the bottom line: I have to send some sort of message about the students' abilities as writers to the university, to the college, to the department, to the parents, and to the students themselves. I still need a benchmark; I still need a rubric. My rubric, however, must present criteria from a different perspective. I don't want to focus on individual papers; I want to focus on the basic level of ability I see overall. Criteria, therefore, change.

57

DETERMINING CRITERIA

In some cases, principally at the elementary or junior-high school level, teachers can involve their students in establishing the criteria for evaluation. I know of one seventh-grade teacher who does just that; she and the students work together to develop a rubric that defines the quality of work in the portfolios for her class. Students reflect on that rubric, assign themselves a grade and explanation for it, and the teacher takes that reflection into account as she evaluates the portfolio, too.

However, in large college-level composition programs teachers may be constrained by a programmatic or departmental criteria; this is true in my case (see Sample 4.1, below and next page).

Sample 4.1: Departmental Grading Rubric for ENGL 0110

The "C" paper carries out the assignment in a **competent** way. The C paper advances a reasonable thesis and offers some relevant support, but expresses them in vague generalities or predictable and conventional ways. The pattern of organization is recognizable to the reader but may be formulaic or may not be the best for the purpose or audience of the paper. The voice and tone are generally appropriate. The style is essentially readable: there are few awkward sentences, few serious errors in wording, and few, if any, glaring errors in grammar and mechanics. The C paper typically relies on merely simple sentence structure, transitions are often weak or formulaic, and word choice may be imprecise or clichéd.

The "B" paper goes **beyond a competent response** to the assignment in several ways. The thesis reflects some originality or excites the curiosity of the audience. The development includes substantive support that is specific, interesting, relevant, and complete. The organization is clear, coherent, and well suited to purpose and audience. Sentence structure shows variety, diction is well suited to audience and purpose, and the transitions function effectively to give the paper unity. The essay is generally free of distracting errors in grammar and mechanics.

Sample 4.1: Departmental Grading Rubric (con.)

The "A" paper is an **excellent** paper, an innovative, creative and perceptive response to the assignment in all ways. The purpose is specific, and some depth or breadth of insight marks the clearly focused thesis. The support is not only interesting and relevant but boldly thought-provoking as well. The careful organization is not only markedly clear and coherent, but also reflects a particularly apt response to the rhetorical situation. The style demonstrates the high competence of the B paper as well as exhibiting finesse through the writer's skillful use of stylistic elements to achieve specific goals. This paper exhibits an exceptionally sophisticated style and mature vocabulary beyond the high rhetorical competence of the B paper.

The "D" paper is one that **begins** to meet the requirements of the assignment, but is flawed in one or more of the following ways. The purpose may be confused or too general. The thesis may not be limited enough or clear enough. The support offered may not be specific, wholly accurate, or relevant but in any case is far from sufficient. The organization may be unclear or confusing. The voice and tone may be inconsistent or somewhat inappropriate. And the style makes it difficult for the reader to understand what is being said. The sentence structure is at times awkward; the word choice is vague or ambiguous; and the number of grammatical or mechanical mistakes is sufficient to be distracting to the reader.

The "F" paper does not meet the requirements of the assignment or is **seriously flawed in one or more** of the following: purpose, support, organization, voice and tone, or style. The severity of a single flaw, or a combination of distracting flaws, renders the paper essentially ineffective. Among the most serious flaws are: a lack of a purpose and/or lack of a controlling thesis that is clear, suitably limited, and on the assigned topic; almost total lack of support; absence of any apparent organizational or developmental plan; a voice or tone that alienates the audience; or a style that is unreadable either because of vagueness and imprecision or because of the number and magnitude of deviations from the conventions of edited American English.

Because of other constraints (articulation agreements, departmental concerns, etc.) we must also use a specific formula for determining a student's final grade: 80% of the final grade must be based on the grades of the major papers required by the program. The remaining 20% must include the grade on a university-mandated final exam.

Teachers who use this rubric have solid basis for grading papers, but must develop procedure for determining final course grades. Some are simple enough: 80% and four major papers = 20% per paper; 10% on the final; 10% on "other." But I have seen some teachers develop procedures on grading papers and determining final grades both that would tax even the best mathematicians: 20% per paper, but 10% of that 20% is having the draft; 5% is grammar; 5% is mechanics, making three separate mathematical equations to solve before assigning a grade! I've already confessed to being math-challenged, and besides, I'd rather spend the time those teachers devote to math to reading and talking about a student's writing. And, I'm not sure that the departmental rubric even supports such a complex system for determining a grade on a single paper.

> ### PS
> Our GTAs have developed an interesting means of using the rubric to grade papers: They copy it, highlight the portions that describe what they see in their evaluation, and return it with the paper. Students seeing most of the criteria for a C highlighted have some interesting feedback to consider.

To be able to use portfolio evaluation, I needed to demonstrate to the department as well as to students that the work they do in my class will be evaluated using the same basic criteria as anyone else's. As a compromise, I have developed a rubric (see Sample 4.2, page 61 and 62) describing the contents of a portfolio that includes the daily work, the major papers.

Sample 4.2: My portfolio grading rubric

PORTFOLIO GRADING RUBRIC – ENGL 0110

A "C" portfolio –<u>All</u> daily work was done on time; there is an indication that the writer tried to find some meaning/usefulness in each one. I see a minimal effort to learn; I see minimal attempts to meet the goals of the course.

The final drafts of the major papers <u>all</u> demonstrate the writer's ability to address rhetorical situations competently. There is adequate support of a recognizable point. The organization is logical but may at times be formulaic or not appropriate for the audience. Transitions are part of that organization, though they may be formulaic in nature. The tone and style are appropriate. The papers are readable; the reader doesn't encounter awkward sentence structures or wording. There are few errors in usage and mechanics.

A grade of "C" means that your writing is "good" in the sense that you are able to write at the basic level of competency expected of you by the University.

A "B" portfolio – <u>All</u> daily work was done on time; there is a greater indication that the writer not only tried to find some meaning/usefulness but also attempted to make connections to his/her own situation. I see a greater effort to learn. I see some evidence of efforts to meet his/her stated goals as well as the goals of the course.

The final drafts of the major papers <u>all</u> demonstrate the writer's ability to address rhetorical situations in some means beyond mere competency. The writing goes beyond the basics in the following ways: the point is original and/or more exciting for the reader; the organization is and the transitions are more sophisticated and the support offered is more substantive and/or relevant. The style and tone reflect more attention to rhetorical concerns and the readers' needs; there is a more sophisticated sentence structure, etc. The work if free of distracting errors.

A grade of "B" means that your writing is better than good in the sense that you are able to write at a level higher than the basic one expected of you.

Sample 4.2: My portfolio rubric (con.)

An "A" portfolio – <u>All</u> daily work was done on time; there is a clear indication that the writer found meaning/usefulness and at the same time connected the information to his/her own situation. I see evidence of a serious effort to meet his/her own stated goals as well as the goals of the course.

The final drafts of the major papers <u>**all**</u> demonstrate the writer's ability to address rhetorical situations in innovative, creative, and perceptive ways. The writing goes beyond "better." The purpose is distinguished by some depth or breadth of insight; all support offered is interesting, relevant, and boldly thought-provoking. The organization is not only coherent, but marked by an appropriateness to the specific rhetorical situation. The writing exhibits finesse on the writer's part in matters of style, diction, etc. There are no errors.

A "D" portfolio – Not all daily work was completed &/or some work was late; the effort to learn is in most cases perfunctory (i.e., you did it just to have something to turn in). The papers all indicate the writer's ability to address rhetorical situations somewhat competently in most cases, but the writing contains weaknesses and/or errors that mark it as less that what is expected.

An "F" portfolio: Less than half of the assigned daily work was completed. The final drafts of the papers indicate the writer's inability to address rhetorical situations in a successful manner.

You might notice something different about the order of the grades described on both the rubrics, too: each begins with the description of a C paper or portfolio and moves to the B and A descriptions after that. This bottom up approach is something else students need to see early, have explained, and understand: what I expect them to do is what a C represents. Unlike many of their high school teachers, I expect to get a paper that "has nothing wrong with it," in their language. That's what a C portfolio demonstrates: the ability to write at a competent level every time. But thanks to the highly inflated, top-down grading practices in most high schools, students come to college with very inflated senses of their own abilities, and we must spend time discussing this new perspective.

Does my rubric work? For me, yes, and the department has approved it. I can and do focus on the degree of writing ability I see in the major papers (including the final exam essay) the students submit; I use the quality of the daily work, effort, and everything else to add a plus or minus to the final grade. Can the students apply it fairly? Yes, once I get them used to the bottom-up perspective and convince them that what got them an A in high school is the basic ability we expect in college, and that is what a C means.

IMPORTANCE OF STUDENT REFLECTION AND SELF-EVALUATION IN PORTFOLIO EVALUATION

There is, however, one key to ensuring portfolios work that is not evident in most other grading procedures: On-going assessment of his/her own work is absolutely necessary. When students are asked to reflect on their own efforts, they tend to feel more invested, more trusted, more engaged, and less victimized by the system. Teachers have developed several means of ensuring on-going student reflection and evaluation.

> **PS**
>
> One of my favorite means of achieving this is to start each conference by asking, "So what do you think of this paper? Is it done? What do you think it needs?" Having to tell me the answers puts the responsibility for the writing back on them, not me. They don't particularly like it, but they end up having to accept the responsibility.

63

Informal Means

Every teacher will have his or her own favorite means of offering students the opportunity to reflect on their work, but I have found the most popular to be these:

> **Process memos** — due with each draft or revision, detailing the writer's goals, reflecting on his/her efforts, successes, and perceptions of strengths and weaknesses;

> **Completion memo** — due as a cover memo to each paper in the final portfolio, again detailing the writer's goals, reflecting on the strengths and weaknesses in the paper;

> **Regular conferences** — scheduled bi-weekly, in which the student updates the teacher on his/her progress.

I've used each of these methods, and each works to a certain extent, depending upon the make-up of each particular class. I tended to prefer the process memo since it allows a more formal, distant voice and perspective; it also serves as a reminder to the student that he/she can't put everything off until the end of the term. But I must admit, I felt badly about using the process memo; I felt too much like Big Brother, peering over the student's shoulder, nagging about getting things done.

Conferences are better, because we can always cover more material and even discuss revision plans and options. I admit I find them challenging from a time standpoint when I have fifty or more composition students in one term. Even if I cancelled office hours and only spent ten minutes

PS
Another earlier point bears repeating: I can do this many conferences only because I have trained myself to read the papers the night before, jot key word notes, and rely on my short-term memory.

with each student, I'd still be spending over twelve hours a week conferencing. That takes too much time away from class preparation unless I am sure students have something else to work on. And, I know that GTAs involved in taking courses and trying to write dissertations can't devote that much time to conferencing. However, I've decided it is time well-spent, so I do conduct conferences more than most.

Because no one method addresses my needs, student needs, and even the practical limitations of time, I tend to assign frequent process memos in the form of a freewrite journal entry and make sure I get an update during each conference I have with a student.

> *PS*
> If I don't get conference I for some reason, I have students write a quick "Dear Dr. Mac, here's how things are going" journal entry; these tell me where and how I can help if I also encourage them to share questions and concerns.

More Formal Measures

Because our program asks us to make sure students have some graded work completed before mid-term (so they can drop the class without penalty should they wish), I require students to write a **midterm profile** and **self-evaluation;** we discuss both, as well as the contents of the portfolio, in a **mid-term conference.** We take two to three days off, depending on the number of students I have any given term; they work on the profile and self-evaluation in class one day, and I cancel classes for the conference on the next one or two days (And though they are not in class, they have homework of some sort to do to prepare for the first day back.).

Each of these three aspects of self-evaluation allows us to evaluate their work in the course from a different perspective. The *profile* asks them to reflect on what they have done, what they have learned, what problems they have encountered, and how they are trying to address them. This globalization of the work done in the course allows them to somewhat distance themselves from the work itself, seeing the overall instead of the specific. The profile is an informal piece, usually a letter to us (the student and me), and intended to help students generalize their efforts before having to look at their work from another perspective. It provides a transition for them, one that helps move from the writer's perspective to the reader's perspective.

The *self-evaluation* (see Sample 4.3, p. 67) asks them to share their judgments on their efforts and the quality of the work they have produced so far from a more traditional standpoint. I ask students to grade themselves in certain areas, including the quality of the papers in progress. I ask them to use the rubric we discussed the first day of class to do this.

I collect the portfolio, review everything in it, read their profile and self-evaluation, and add my evaluation of their work on the same sheet they filled out. In the conference, we discuss where our evaluations match and where they don't and why, negotiating our understanding of terms and degrees of effort and success.

> **PS**
>
> In a 15-minute mid-term conference, I can usually discuss the grade, explain that the grade represents the work as it is now, and use the most recent paper to discuss the kinds of revisions the writer will want to consider if he or she wants a higher grade. It isn't fun, I'll admit, but it is important.

Sample 4.3: Midterm self-evaluation form

MID-TERM SELF-EVALUATION
Please respond to the following on this sheet.
(Yes: you must give yourself a grade in each area.)

Use the following scale to grade yourself in each area below:

> F = not putting in any effort at this point
> D = effort is merely perfunctory
> C = doing enough to get by
> B = trying and taking advantage of some opportunities
> A = lots of effort & taking advantage of every opportunity

_____ Effort on homework (includes submitting work on time)

_____ Effort at working daily on writing

_____ Effort on drafting papers

_____ Effort at revising papers

_____ Effort at becoming a good responder in groups

Review the rubric for evaluation I gave you the first day, then give yourself a grade in each area below. Please give us an honest evaluation of your work **as it is right now**, not a prediction of what it will become.

_____ Grade for "Other" (in class, homework, effort on drafting, revisions, etc.) Comments:

_____ Grade for Essay 1, short papers 1 & 2, and pre-work/draft for Essay 2 – **together**, not as separate papers. Comments:

_____ **Based on all of the above, what grade would you give yourself for the course right now?** If you are not pleased with this grade, what do you think you need to do to improve it?

Do I have the same success the first grade teacher I mentioned earlier does? No, I'm sorry to say. What I usually discover is that while some students have a solid sense of how well they have done, other students are still working from the top-down model of grading they are used to from high school. That is, their logic goes something like this: "If there is nothing wrong with the paper, it is an A paper. You haven't told me there is anything wrong with my paper, so I must be making an A."

Although we have discussed the fact that "nothing wrong" is what we expect at the college level, and that is the basic criteria that describe C-level work, students still don't understand. I don't think they are stubborn and just refuse to accept the idea. I think it far more likely that they have never encountered the bottom up approach to writing before. After all, they have experienced twelve (or more) years of top down grading and are even still experiencing it in chemistry and math courses.

But they must deal with it. When I ask, they usually say no, they didn't really read the rubric; they just went on what their other teachers would have done. That lets me know I need to make more of an effort at explaining the rubric and the bottom-up approach we need to take to evaluating writing. Or, they

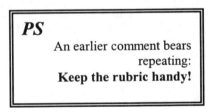

PS

An earlier comment bears repeating:
Keep the rubric handy!

say they have assigned the grade to the papers they *intend* to write, not the drafts in their current state. That's when we have the discussion of what gets graded, and I explain again that the text as it is presented on the page is what gets evaluated. Both of these kinds of students inevitably give themselves a grade at least one level higher than I do; some whom I evaluate at the C level award themselves an A. Explaining the difference once again, on a one-to-one level, is all most need to understand how I use the rubric.

I won't lie: mid-term conferences can be stressful for both the students and me. Nothing hurts me more than having to tell someone that I could not put down an A based on what I read in her portfolio; students who have seen positive comments as well as suggestions for revisions on papers are crushed to hear the work is only at the C level at this point.

In one sense, we can both feel betrayed. I feel betrayed when it seems that the student has not made the effort to seriously consider the importance of the goals of the course and the rubric. The student can feel betrayed because she thinks I have made contradictory comments; she thought that because I made positive comments, I liked what she was doing; now, it seems to her that I'm saying it isn't good enough because I have not assigned the portfolio the A she feels she deserves.

When I remind them that mid-term grades don't count, that the grade is not something that gets averaged in with something else at the end of the term, we can begin negotiating revision needs and addressing the issue of effort. The mid-term grade becomes merely a crude evaluation of the work the student has done during the first half of the course, a chance for us to see if we are working from the same standpoint, and a chance for the student to determine whether he or she should consider dropping the course. In many cases, it is useful for motivating students to work harder on revisions and the papers yet to be assigned, but I admit I hate using it that way.

> **PS**
>
> Let's face it: Someone is always going to get upset and cry, so keep a box of tissues handy. And, someone will get angry. Learning to be patient, to listen to the student's comments may help more in the long run. More often than not, I discover some outside influence is the source of that anger. When I do, I propose we talk about how to address that situation so the student can focus on his writing. But don't if you know you will uncomfortable doing so.

PORTFOLIOS AND THE FINAL EXAM

Our program mandates a final exam, one that students complete without our help, demonstrating the skills they have learned during the term; however, it is not a departmental exam (e.g., we do not all give the same prompt, we do not grade each other's students, both practices typical of programs with a departmental exam). The only programmatic requirement is that it be progressive in nature (e.g., students work on it over two or three class periods, practicing the writing process they have been using) and that they finish it during the scheduled exam period. Teachers in our program who use portfolio evaluation approach the final from different perspectives.

I assign 2 short papers as the final exam: an essay that duplicates the kinds of papers they have been working on in class and a final self-evaluation in either the form of a brief essay (see Sample 4.5, p. 71) or in the form of a letter (see Sample 4.6, p. 72). Each asks that they present their argument for a grade after they have had the chance to reflect on changes and revisions they have made since mid-term. I ask the students to reflect on some of the same information I ask for at mid-term, but I also change the focus of the self-evaluation to the quality that the final papers represent overall. I usually find that they have a much better sense of what the rubric says and their own abilities by the end of the quarter; most propose the grade I eventually report for them. But I also face the disappointment of realizing that some never did catch on; a handful still assign themselves an A because they "did everything you told me to."

Sample 4.4: Final Self-evaluation: Essay version

Exam Essay 2:
This is the second short piece you will write as part of the final exam. It is to be an essay, not as polished or developed as Exam 1 is, probably. You will begin it today by reading through your portfolio material and generating ideas. You won't be able to draft this one or even finish it until the exam period because your portfolio is not complete yet. But you can begin thinking about what points you want to make in your paper and identifying specific examples from what you remember.

You need to spend the entire class period on this piece today. Tomorrow you will do the course evaluation during the first 20 minutes or so, then you may work on whichever piece you wish.

Assignment for Exam 2:
Discuss the significance of what you have learned about writing during the past 10 weeks: where did you start? How far have you come? What grade does your final portfolio deserve – and why? How did you get to this point? What will you do with this knowledge and experience? How will you use all this in the future? Reflect on all the work you've done (journals, reader responses, prewriting, drafts, peer responses, revisions – anything we have done).

This is to be an <u>essay</u> with a <u>point</u> for the <u>reader</u> (in this case, me) – part of it should involve self-evaluation and an argument for the grade you think your portfolio deserves. I **<u>strongly</u>** suggest reviewing the grading rubric before beginning this essay.

Special Constraints:
No 5-paragraph, formulaic essays.
"I worked really hard" is NOT an argument that will convince me of anything. I don't want to read that comment or one similar to it in your essay.

Sample 4.5: Final Profile in letter form: Sample questions

In a letter to us, briefly discuss the following:

1. Read the piece you wrote the second day of class (Journal 2; the response to the Harris essay). How have your writing and your process changed since the beginning of the quarter? Which aspect of your process gives you the most trouble?

2. In general, how do you feel about what you've written this term? What do you see as your strengths and weaknesses? What especially do you think you should continue to work on?

Spend more time considering/answering these next two; yes, your response will be a factor in my evaluation of your work.

3. Discuss **each** of the major papers you've been working on: What are the strengths and weaknesses of the final draft of **each**? What about writing did each teach you - and how? Which did you enjoy writing the most and why? The least?

4. **Briefly** comment on the strengths and weaknesses of the short papers. Which was hardest & why? Easiest & why? Most beneficial?

5. **Based on the rubric**: What grade would you give the final drafts (<u>overall – not individually</u>—including the final essay) of your papers? What grade would you give the rest of the work (keep attendance, etc. in mind, too). What grade would you give yourself for the course and why?

and YES, you must give yourself a grade.
Base the grade you propose on the descriptions in the rubric.

Angela has an interesting variation on the final that some teachers might like better. She has her students write an essay that accomplishes two basic goals: an introduction to the portfolio and an argument for the grade they think it deserves (see Sample 4.6, p. 74). Students in her class must read each paper again, closely, looking for and even citing evidence of the characteristics they claim the papers in their portfolio demonstrate.

THE PROCESS OF EVALUATING THE PORTFOLIO

Once I have the complete portfolio, once I have the final exam essay and self-evaluation letter, what do I do? How do I actually determine the students' final grades for the course? The answer is simple but deceptive: I read.

I've already prepared an evaluation worksheet (see Sample 4.7, p. 75) and after reviewing my journal page for the student whose portfolio I pick up first, I page through it, checking to make sure everything I asked to be included is submitted. I then separate the final drafts of the papers from their drafts. I put them in the order they were written, and I start reading.

> ### PS
> I collect the portfolio at the exam period; this gives my students several extra days to finish it. I have less time to read, but I am prepared for that. Angela, on the other hand, collects portfolios on the last day of class, giving her more time to read. She often has all the portfolios read by the exam period. All she has to do is read the final essay and determine the final grade.

Sample 4. : Angela's final exam essay introducing the portfolio

Insenga / EH 110 / Final Exam
We've made it to the end of the quarter. It's time to prepare for your last writing assignment for me. Here's what you will need:

1.   Your diagnostic (I'll hand this out)
2.   Two of your four graded essays
3.   Your journal
4.   A few freewrites
5.   The drafting, peer review, organization, grammar, and writing abilities you have fostered this quarter.

What you'll need to do with these documents: First, you'll need to sit down and read your own writing, my comments, your peer review partners' comments. You may want to lake notes on how you have/haven't improved, on how peer review helped/has not helped, on how you've acquired a new writing skill, etc.

Next, you'll want to begin thinking about your own evolution as a writer. You may ask yourself, "How have I improved?" or 'Why have I improved?' You can ask questions like "What's my strongest asset as a writer?" or "What would I like my future teachers to focus on in my own writing?" You can comment on the value of freewrites, journal entries, or the essays themselves. There are many other things you may choose to focus on here, as well; it's up to you. There are many roads that lead to Rome. Just remember, the main idea for this final is for you to discuss, candidly, your evolution as a composition student Focus on the positive as well as the places where you stumbled

For your own ethos, you may want to quote your own papers, or use my comments or peer review partners' to support your claims about your writing. Your logos here will be the essay format. You may find it useful to use "because" or "If . . . then" structures to discuss your evolution as a writer. Your pathos can also appear in variety of ways; what assignment meant the most to you and why, what your favorite kind of writing was and why, if any skills you have learned here will or will not apply to that "real world." Like I said before, this final is not meant to psych you out; on the contrary, it's a chance for you to show your stuff, for you to comment on your own evolution as a writer using the very skills you have acquired. Your subject here is YOU. Self-reflection is the name of this game. Good luck folks.

Sample 4.7: My grading worksheet

ENGL 0110 101 Fall 1999	AB	HW	P	SE	F	KMC	Final Grade
Brown, Bobby	-2	✓	✓	B	✓	B/c	B -
Christianson, Joe	-1	✓	✓				
Davis, Peggy	-5	-3	✓				
Ethridge, Jane	-0	✓+	✓				
Frank, Tom	-1	✓	✓				
Jones, Celeste	-11	-10	X	X	X	X	FA
Etc . . .							
		ol 12					

I begin with the letter of self-evaluation. Why? I want to read the final papers within the context the student has offered them; that is, I want to keep in mind what the student says about the papers as I read them.

As I read the final drafts of the essays (first) then the final exam essay (keeping in mind it did not have all the same opportunities for development the rest of the portfolio papers did), I might make check marks in the margins where I notice some evidence of a point the student made in the self-evaluation about strengths or weaknesses. But essentially, I just read. After I have read the entire set of papers I list for myself the strengths and weaknesses I noticed throughout my reading. I keep the rubric in front of me, referring to it often to remind myself of the relative importance of certain elements. And, by the end of this process, I can identify the letter grade that best describes the writing ability I see in that student's papers.

Then I quickly review the FWRs and journals and other work in the portfolio, paying attention to the drafts and comments other students made on them. Sounds easy, right? On one level it is: All I do is read, holistically, using the rubric as a guide. But on another level it isn't an easy task at all; I'm constantly noticing where in papers students did or didn't revise something we discussed, where errors (that I marked on drafts) did or didn't get corrected, where some suggestion a peer or I made was or was not incorporated.

How am I able to do this? Thanks in part to my journal pages I have a record (cryptic, admittedly) of these points (a good short-term memory helps, too). I have also learned to train my short-term memory to retain information; all I need is a key word to trigger an idea, suggestion, error, or question that I discussed with that students (Sometimes my memory of what the students wrote is better than theirs, especially when they are not particularly invested in the papers or the course. It is, I agree, a depressing realization, but often true.).

If I have done a good job of explaining portfolio evaluation to the class, if I have done a good job of explaining the rubric, if the students have actively participated and honestly evaluated their work, we usually come to the same conclusion about the final grade. How often does that happen? By the final exam, it occurs more often than not; I'd estimate that at least 85% of my students accurately assess their abilities. However, some students will insist on awarding themselves a higher grade "because I tried real hard" or because "I did everything you told me to do." Those are the students who never got it, never figured out that I don't play either of those games, who never took responsibility for their own work. Thankfully, however, the difference is usually only one letter; they will propose Bs, but I'll see C-level portfolios instead.

THE BOTTOM LINE

For me, the advantage of being able to teach the way I need to far outweighs the disadvantage of having so many portfolios to read at the end of the term. But I won't mislead you: reading and fairly evaluating that much does get tedious, especially since our registrar demands we submit grades within forty-eight hours (I never am able to meet this deadline). My trick to surviving and making sure I do the best job I can? I take breaks (usually three portfolios at one sitting is the maximum I try to complete), read holistically, prepare the evaluation worksheet ahead of time, and consciously refer to the rubric during the entire session. That's best advice I can share.

CHAPTER 5

ELECTRONIC PORTFOLIOS

You won't find much in the literature about electronic portfolios before 1988; in fact, only a handful (relatively, that is) of instructors have ventured into this newest incarnation of portfolio evaluation. However, with computer literacy becoming a concern and a goal, with the funds being designated specifically for equipment purchases and support, with the advent and explosion of the resources available on the World Wide Web and, more recently, thanks to WYSIWYG programs (what-you-see-is-what-you-get; programs that write HTML code), electronic portfolios are becoming easy enough to be practical and useful. In just the last three years, electronic portfolios have become one of the most discussed topics in the literature.

What are electronic portfolios? They don't differ in content that much from paper ones; electronic portfolios still represent a body of work by a writer. However, the presentation of the material is usually quite different. Students have the chance to write more than just the traditional paper; they can enhance their work with graphics, photographs, and even links to additional on-line information. In some cases, the development of the webpage itself, both writing it and designing it, is becoming part of the writing curriculum.

THE EASIEST VERSION

Perhaps the easiest electronic portfolio is merely the paperless one; instead of a folder of paper, the student submits a disk with all his or her work on it. Or, if you have access to a server, the student can FTP files or papers to an account the teacher has set up. Each teacher I know handles it a bit differently, but usually each file is labeled according to the teacher's direction; she can then sit at her terminal, call up papers and read them, and even place them in multiple windows for comparison.

The advantage to this version is fairly obvious: no storage space considerations, no heavy folders full of papers to carry home, no chance of a paper falling out of a folder and getting lost. But there are disadvantages, too. Students might not have followed instructions, causing the teacher to have to search for specific papers; the disk might be corrupt with a virus; or the disk could get damaged. Or, the server might go down, preventing the teacher from accessing the students' work.

Folder-Based Options

Teachers familiar with the computer environment will find setting up some kind of folder system relatively easy to do. All you need is a server capable of supporting a network and storing several pieces of writing for each student. Some commercial programs simplify this process, providing file systems for teachers and students, options for tailoring it to individual teacher or course needs, and even providing support programs for response and chat opportunities. For this version, portfolio contents are often cached in folders that are stored on a departmental or even university server.

One typical format of the folder-based portfolio is for the student to cache all the work for each certain assignment in a separate folder; perhaps the teacher will ask for all final papers to be cached in yet a different one. Some sort of introductory file is included, along with a directory describing the contents of each folder.

I can't speak for Mac users, but the Windows environments (Windows 95 and Windows 98) make this version quite easy to maintain. All the viewer (teacher or student) needs is a work-processing program that will allow him or her to read the contents of the folders. Saving each text as a .txt file will insure any user of being able to read any given file. During the term, when students need access to each other's papers for discussion and response, I would probably set up a file system like this one:

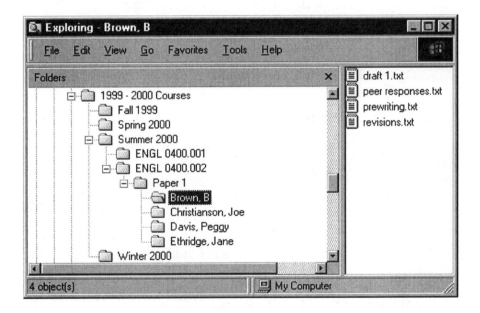

Later, for evaluation purposes, I would probably have students move the final drafts of their papers into a file system that looks like this:

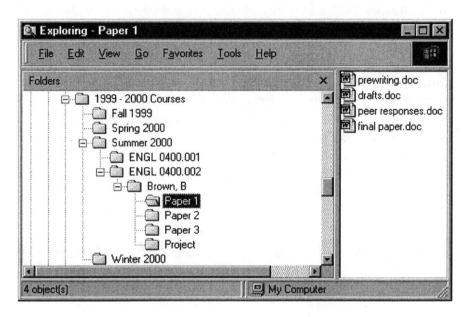

With both formats, my students should be able to save work written in any word-processing program they have available to them; I should be able to read any given text in the program I am most comfortable using. Only formatting issues are problematic since some formatting is not saved in the .txt file.

Formatting issues are easily resolved if students can use the same work-processing program. Computers in our classroom are both loaded with MS WORD and Corel Word Perfect, each of which is, thankfully, fairly easy to convert to the other.

WEB-BASED PORTFOLIOS

What is usually meant when someone mentions electronic portfolios is a web-based one. Thanks to the plethora of programs available, students can easily produce a portfolio for a course by caching papers in specific folders designated for his or her class or even establishing a web page that allows them to publish the contents of their portfolio on the World Wide Web.

The page can be as simple as an on-line offering of the text of an essay or report, to a page that incorporates graphics, photos, and even links to resources.

SPECIAL DEMANDS OF ELECTRONIC PORTFOLIOS

Teachers interested in implementing an electronic portfolio system in their classrooms have had to come to terms with equipment, personal knowledge, and even curriculum demands. I confess: I have yet to fully implement such a system. Let me share the thinking I have been working through in each of these areas as I try to decide whether electronic portfolios will work for me.

Equipment Concerns

First, I have to make sure I can offer each student opportunities equal to all other students in my class; this means, I need to have a computer with the appropriate software available for everyone. I had to consider the following:

- ❑ What kind of equipment (Mac or IBM platform?) is available to me?

- ❑ How many machines can I count on using?

- How often can I use these machines for my class?

- Can students use the equipment at any time or only during class?

- Is the equipment compatible with the machines the students have access to?

- Is there adequate server support for electronic portfolios?

- Is there adequate technical support?

I am lucky. Our department has two computer classrooms designed specifically for writing courses. I have access to one and which it is doesn't matter; the equipment in each is nearly identical. A network linking the machines in each room to each other makes moving between rooms easy. Each room contains enough computers that my students could each have their own machine to work on. Each computer is capable of running the software I would be interested in using, and each computer is compatible with systems available in the university's open computer labs.

Scheduling use of the rooms is usually not a problem; I can use either room as often as twice a week if I want to. However, the rooms are available to the entire faculty, and we must negotiate and share. The department typically offers over seventy-five sections of composition, technical, and business writing classes each term, which, of course, limits the number of classes and teachers able to

> **PS**
> If you are not comfortable in the computer classroom environment, students won't be either. You might warm up to electronic portfolios by using a computer classroom on a regular basis. It's good for the students to have the chance to learn to compose at the keyboard, too, something I think will become of the norm (at least it has for me).

84

use the computer classroom. At any given class time during the day, as many as twelve different teachers have the right to request use of the rooms. Again, I am lucky; I am one of a handful of teachers interested in using the computer classrooms.

Though the university has set up several computer labs on campus that are open to students twenty-four hours a day, and though some students own their own equipment, the students do not have access to our special classroom-based network outside of the classroom setting; everything they do has to be saved to a disk so they can work on it outside of the computer classroom environment.

Technical support is not an issue I need to be concerned with; I know enough to troubleshoot basic problems. In addition, two other faculty members serve as resource contacts; they are available to help me troubleshoot problems I cannot solve on my own. And the university computing division is only a phone call away should I need immediate support.

So far, so good: I have the physical resources of machines and support available to me, but I might face some minor accessibility issues.

Knowledge Concerns

What about my knowledge level? Assuming I want students to be able to produce and maintain their own web pages, can I honestly say I could teach them to do so? Yes and no: I have designed, written, and published web pages, but I can't claim to be an expert when it comes to writing HTML code. I understand the basics well enough to troubleshoot and solve minor problems, but not much else. I am comfortable using WYSIWYG programs; I could teach students the basics of the ones available for our use.

What about the students' knowledge levels? Do they understand the basics of how the WWW works, what a webpage is, and are they even interested in learning about these if they don't? Right now, most of my students seem to be somewhat web savvy; that is, each can find his or her way around the web to a certain extent. I have a couple of students who already maintain their own web pages; our university, which has moved into the virtual world for everything from registration to posting grades, provides server space for every student (and faculty) interested in maintaining personal web pages.

However, some of my students don't seem to know much about the web; some have confessed they don't even like using computers. And believe it or not, I have a few students who have never used a computer. Requiring a web-based portfolio of them would mean I put them at a distinct disadvantage.

Currently, given the limited accessibility of equipment and the lack of knowledge and experience of some students, I think I would be able to implement at most a modified folder-based electronic portfolio system on our classroom network. I will have to do some extra instruction about computers and folder systems to make the situation fair for all. But, what about the departmental curriculum requirements? Will I be able to include this extra instruction?

Curriculum Concerns

Given that I have a programmatic curriculum I am responsible for teaching, I probably should have started my thinking here. Can I meet all the course goals and still have time to teach enough computer skills to fairly implement even a network folder based portfolio system?

On one level, the answer is no: the programmatic curriculum does not allow for much other than writing formal academic writing. Teaching HTML code writing and designing web pages would make demands on the students that far exceed the stated requirements of the course. And, since so many of my students don't know the basics of HTML or even the WWW, these requirements could constitute an extra burden.

I think, too, that including these elements of web authoring could take the focus away from the stated goals of the course. Right now I cannot demonstrate how learning to design, author, and maintain a webpage will teach students the nuances of academic exposition, argument, and research. This reason alone prevents me from fully implementing an electronic portfolio system. Our program requirements, the lack of resources for all students, and the limitations of the curriculum means that our program is just too traditionally paper oriented for that. I will have to continue to use portfolios as I have been until the curriculum catches up with the electronic and virtual world.

But that will happen; some composition courses are including web page design and maintenance as part of the curriculum goals under the guise of teaching audience analysis and writing directed at specific audiences. That might work for some of the papers my students write, but not all.

THE BOTTOM LINE FOR ME

For now, I can only dream about electronic portfolios; there are too many disadvantages and impediments for me to consider using them. Because I know I want to and need to focus on the basic rhetorical constraints of writing within the academy, I know I shouldn't add what might look like frivolous concerns to the course goals. Yes, it would be nice for everyone to develop his or her own webpage, but I am not ready to give up class time to teach HTML code or even webpage design issues. Far too many of my students need to be concerned with developing their ideas with examples and evidence, developing arguments with outside sources responsibly and correctly, and even looking toward sentence combining to improve the prose.

> **PS**
>
> I am going to start small; this summer I will experiment with the server-based electronic folder system and offer a web-page project as an option for students in an advanced composition class. Those sample screen shots I used earlier are my initial ideas about how I will set it up.

When will I revisit the idea of an electronic portfolio, especially a web-based one? When all the students I have write HTML or use WYSIWYG programs as easily as most do the WWW right now, I might be able to implement an electronic portfolio system; I'll have to see whether the extras would fit into the course goals.

THE ADVANTAGES OF ELECTRONIC PORTFOLIOS

To be fair, however, consider these advantages of electronic portfolios:

- ✓ They are (or can be) paperless (fewer trees were killed to pass this course);

- ✓ the work is easy to respond to (I type faster than I write; I can respond much more quickly);

- ✓ they can enhance objectivity (I am not affected by neatness, etc.);

- ✓ they make assignments much more real for students (thus allowing them to invest much more in the course);

- ✓ they afford real publishing opportunities, something paper portfolios rarely (if ever) do;

- ✓ they foster prolific writing (students do write more if the result is real and is posted for the world to see);

- ✓ they allow students to learn skills they may find valuable in the future (many jobs require web and web-page designs now);

- ✓ students are able to experiment with more than just text as they work to present info or argue a point (and graphics might enhance our evaluation sessions, too).

THE DISADVANTAGES OF ELECTRONIC PORTFOLIOS

And there are some:

- ✓ students require access to computer classroom on a regular basis;

- ✓ students need access to machines outside of class, at home, or in the dorms;

- ✓ teachers and students must know the system and how the local network works quite well;

- ✓ teachers will have to teach webpage design and may have to teach HTML code writing;

- ✓ the bells and whistles of web design can get in the way and become the aspect that students spend more time on;

- ✓ evaluating the bells and whistles will have to be included in the rubric criteria;

- ✓ imaginative students will excel, but not necessarily learn anything about writing.

I hope you'll consider the advantages and disadvantages carefully as you decide if, when, and how electronic portfolios might work for you.

SELECTED RESOURCES

The following is not by any means comprehensive; instead, I offer a highly eclectic list of sources that have been most useful in my development as a teacher who uses portfolio evaluation at the college level.

BOOKS

Banta, Trudy W. *Assessment in Practice: Putting Principles to Work on College Campuses*. San Francisco: Jossey-Bass, 1996.

Belanoff, Pat and Marcia Dickson, eds. *Portfolios: Process and Product*. Portsmouth, NH: Heineman/Boyntan-Cook, 1991.

> See especially the article by Jeffrey Sommers, "Bringing Practice in Line with Theory: Using Portfolio Grading in the Composition Classroom."

Calfree, Robert C. and Pam Perfumo, eds. *Writing Portfolios in the Classroom: Policy and Practice, Promise and Peril*. Mahwah, NJ: L. Erlbaum Associates, 1996.

Graves, Donald H. and Bonnie S. Sunstein, eds. *Portfolio Portraits*. Portsmouth, NH: Heineman/Boyntan-Cook, 1992.

Hewitt, Geof. *A Portfolio Primer: Teaching, Collecting, and Assessing Student Writing*. Portsmouth, NH: Heineman, 1995.

White, Edward M., William Lutz, and Sandra Kamusikiti, eds. *Assessment of Writing: Politics, Policies, Practices*. New York: Modern Language Association, 1996.

Yancy, Kathleen Blake and Irwin Weiser. *Situating Portfolios: Four Perspectives*. Logan, UT: Utah State University Press, 1997.

Yancy, Kathleen Blake, ed. *Portfolios in the Writing Classroom: An Introduction*. Urbana, IL: NCTE, 1992.

JOURNAL ARTICLES

Hawisher, Gail E. and Cynthia L. Selfe, eds. *Computers in Composition: An International Journal for Teachers of Writing. Special Issue: Electronic Portfolios, Kathleen Blake Yancy, Guest Editor,* 13:2 (1996). Includes the following:

> Forbes, Cheryl. "Cowriting, Overwriting, and Overriding in Portfolio Land Online," pp. 195-205.

> Howard, Rebecca Moore. "Memoranda to Myself: Maxims for the Online Portfolio," pp. 155-167.

> Purves, Alan. "Electronic Portfolios," pp. 135-146.

> Watkins, Steve. "World Wide Web Authoring in the Portfolio-Assessed, (Inter)Networked Composition Course," pp 219-230.

> Yancy, Kathleen Blake. "The Electronic Portfolio: Shifting Paradigms," pp. 259-262.

WEBSITES

Grabill, Jeff. E-Portfolios for Rhetoric & Composition. 1999. Online. Available: <http://www.gsu.edu/~engjtg/Temp/Portfolios/portfoliostart.htm>.

Clayton, Maria A. Computer-assisted, Portfolio-based Composition: The Next Step for Freshman Composition at MTSU. 1998. Online. Available:http://www.mtsu.edu/~itconf/proceed98/mclayton.html>.

POSTSCRIPT

My intent for this book is that it be a decision making guide for you; I hope I have provided enough information as well as my thinking about certain issues to be helpful when you begin to consider and decide whether portfolio evaluation will work for you. Should you find you have additional questions, please don't hesitate to e-mail them to me at <mccleka@mail.auburn.edu>. I'll do my best to address your concerns.